Quality Management

Student Manual

COURSE TECHNOLOGY

THOMSON LEARNING

Australia • Canada • Mexico • Singapore
Spain • United Kingdom • United States

D1226090

Quality Management

VP and GM of Courseware:	Michael Springer
Series Product Managers:	Caryl Bahner-Guhin, Charles G. Blum, and Adam A. Wilcox
Developmental Editor:	Adam A. Wilcox
Project Editor:	Martin Lasater
Series Designer:	Adam A. Wilcox
Cover Designer:	Steve Deschene

For more information contact:

Course Technology
25 Thomson Place
Boston, MA 02210

Or find us on the Web at: www.course.com

For permission to use material from this text or product, contact us by

- Web: www.thomsonrights.com
- Phone: 1-800-730-2214
- Fax: 1-800-730-2215

Trademarks

Course ILT is a trademark of Course Technology.

Some of the product names and company names used in this book have been used for identification purposes only and may be trademarks or registered trademarks of their respective manufacturers and sellers.

Disclaimer

Course Technology reserves the right to revise this publication and make changes from time to time in its content without notice.

ISBN 0-619-07556-2

Printed in the United States of America

1 2 3 4 5 PM 04 03 02 01

Contents

Quality Management

Introduction

After reading this introduction, you will know how to:

A Use Course Technology ILT manuals in general.

B Use a target student description, course objectives, and a skills inventory to properly set your expectations for the course.

Topic A: About the manual

Course Technology ILT philosophy

Course Technology ILT manuals facilitate your learning by providing structured interaction with the subject. While we provide text to explain difficult concepts, the hands-on activities are the focus of our courses. By paying close attention as your instructor leads you through these activities, you will learn the concepts effectively.

We believe strongly in the instructor-led classroom. During class, focus on your instructor. Our manuals are designed and written to facilitate your interaction with your instructor, and not to call attention to the manuals themselves.

We believe in the basic approach of setting expectations, delivering instruction, and providing summary and review afterwards. For this reason, lessons begin with objectives and end with summaries. We also provide overall course objectives and a course summary to provide both an introduction to and closure on the entire course.

Manual components

The manuals contain these major components:

- Table of contents
- Introduction
- Units
- Course summary
- Glossary
- Index

Each element is described below.

Table of contents

The table of contents acts as a learning roadmap.

Introduction

The introduction contains information about our training philosophy and our manual components, features, and conventions. It contains descriptions of the target student, objectives, and setup for the course.

Units

Units are the largest structural component of the course content. A unit begins with a title page that lists objectives for each major subdivision, or topic, within the unit. Within each topic, conceptual and explanatory information alternates with hands-on activities. Units conclude with a summary comprising one paragraph for each topic, and an independent practice activity that gives you an opportunity to practice the skills you've learned.

The conceptual information takes the form of text paragraphs, exhibits, lists, and tables. The activities are structured in two columns, one telling you what to do, the other providing explanations, descriptions, and graphics.

Course summary

This section provides a text summary of the entire course. It is useful for providing closure at the end of the course. The course summary also indicates the next course in this series, if there is one, and lists additional resources you might find useful as you continue to learn about the subject.

Glossary

The glossary provides definitions for all of the key terms used in this course.

Index

The index enables you to quickly find information about a particular topic or concept of the course.

Manual conventions

We've tried to keep the number of elements and the types of formatting to a minimum in the manuals. This aids in clarity and makes the manuals more classically elegant looking. But there are some conventions and icons you should know about.

Convention/Icon	Description
Italic text	In conceptual text, indicates a new term or feature.
Bold text	In unit summaries, indicates a key term or concept. In an independent practice activity, indicates an explicit item that you select, choose, or type.

Hands-on activities

The hands-on activities are the most important parts of our manuals. They are usually divided into two columns, with questions or concepts on the left and answers and explanations on the right. Here's a sample:

Do it!

A-1: Steps for brainstorming

Exercises

1 Sequence the steps for brainstorming.

Begin generating ideas.

Select the purpose.

Organize for the session.

Ask questions and clarify ideas.

Review the rules.

Topic B: Setting your expectations

Properly setting your expectations is essential to your success. This topic will help you do that by providing:

- A description of the target student at whom the course is aimed
- A list of the objectives for the course
- A skills assessment for the course

Target student

The typical students of this course will be managers, supervisors, or team leaders who need to learn how to implement quality measures in order to increase quality within their organization.

Course objectives

These overall course objectives will give you an idea about what to expect from the course. It is also possible that they will help you see that this course is not the right one for you. If you think you either lack the prerequisite knowledge or already know most of the subject matter to be covered, you should let your instructor know that you think you are misplaced in the class.

After completing this course, you will know how to:

- Identify the concepts commonly associated with quality management, the role of management in implementing quality, the steps an organization should follow to incorporate improvements into daily management, the ways in which variation leads to loss, select characteristics of common causes of variation, and identify frequent sources of variation.

- Identify the relationship between quality and cost, identify the benefits of establishing quality requirements for products and services, identify management's responsibilities for achieving conformance, and identify the costs of customer dissatisfaction.

- Identify the characteristics of a customer-oriented organization, the steps for becoming customer oriented, the approaches to conduct customer research, the benefits of a customer-oriented organization, and the financial incentives for developing loyal customers.

- Identify types of flow charts; create and analyze a flow chart, a check sheet, a histogram, and a run chart; and identify characteristics of a control chart.

- Create a cause-and-effect diagram, identify the general categories that can be used as main causes on a cause-and-effect diagram, create a Pareto chart and analyze it, create a scatter diagram and interpret it, create an interrelationship diagram, and identify the root causes.

- Sequence and follow the steps for brainstorming, identify the purpose of affinity diagrams, construct activity network diagrams, and identify the benefits provided by knowing the critical path of a project.

- Identify the goals management should achieve to prepare for leading business process improvement, and sequence the steps for planning improvements.

- Identify the qualifications needed in a process manager, the responsibilities of a process manager, the steps for establishing a process improvement team, the responsibilities of process improvement team members, and use flow charts in business process improvement.

- Identify the elements of a process that a process improvement team should understand, the characteristics of the quality management techniques used to streamline a process, and the aspects of a process that should be measured.

Skills inventory

Use the following form to gauge your skill level entering the class. For each skill listed, rate your familiarity from 1 to 5, with five being the most familiar. *This is not a test.* Rather, it is intended to provide you with an idea of where you're starting from at the beginning of class. If you're wholly unfamiliar with all the skills, you might not be ready for the class. If you think you already understand all of the skills, you might need to move on to the next Module in the series. In either case, you should let your instructor know as soon as possible.

Knowledge and skills	1	2	3	4	5
Concepts commonly associated with quality management					
Role of management in implementing quality, the steps an organization should follow to incorporate improvements into daily management					
Common causes of variation					
Relationship between quality and cost					
Management's responsibilities for achieving conformance					
Characteristics of a customer-oriented organization					
Flow charts, check sheets, histograms, and run charts					
Characteristics of control charts					
Cause-and-effect diagrams					
Pareto charts					
Scatter diagrams					
Interrelationship diagrams and identifying root causes					
Steps for brainstorming					
Affinity diagrams					
Construct activity network diagrams					
Critical path of a project					
Goals of management in preparing for leading business process improvement					

Knowledge and skills	1	2	3	4	5
Process managers and their responsibilities					
Process improvement teams					
Responsibilities of process improvement team members					
Flow charts in business process improvement					
Elements of a process that a process improvement team should understand					
Quality management techniques used to streamline a process					
Aspects of a process that should be measured					

Topic C: Reviewing the course

No special preparation is needed for you to review this course on your own.

Unit 1

Fundamentals of quality management

Unit time: 30 minutes

Complete this unit, and you'll know how to:

A Identify the concepts commonly associated with quality management, the role of management in implementing quality, and the steps an organization should follow to incorporate improvements into daily management.

B Identify the ways in which variation leads to loss, select characteristics of common causes of variation, and identify frequent sources of variation.

Topic A: Defining quality management

Explanation

Quality management is the process, directed by upper management, through which a company continuously tries to improve the quality of workmanship, processes, and products. The primary aim of quality management is to organize project planning, product design, and program implementation such that resulting products and services are available to customers at a high quality and reasonable cost.

Some of the concepts commonly associated with quality management include the following:

- Ensuring customer satisfaction by integrating the customer's needs into strategic planning.
- Improving continuously by finding ways to make processes work better.
- Shifting attitudes, so organizational and individual successes are viewed as a result of teamwork and collaboration.
- Empowering people by providing training, encouraging personal initiative, and giving recognition.
- Providing managerial leadership by example.

Individuals who led the Quality movement

Joseph M. Juran, W. Edwards Deming, and Philip B. Crosby led the Quality movement that came about in the United States in the 1980s. By the time American companies became interested in quality management, Deming, Juran, and Crosby already had considerable experience in the quality field and had developed their own approaches to quality management.

Deming is noted for having led the Quality movement in Japan in the 1950s. He presented his approach to quality management in a 14-point program. Deming felt management had to commit itself to a process of continual improvement by acquiring the resources needed to support improvement, building quality into work processes, and giving workers a clear definition of acceptable work.

Deming also created a cycle for improvement known as the Deming Cycle for Improvement, which calls for project planning, team member training, efficient activity execution, verification that activities meet project goals, and documentation of lessons learned. Another name for this cycle is the Plan-Do-Check-Act Cycle, as shown in Exhibit 1-1.

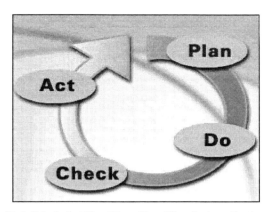

Exhibit 1-1: The Plan-Do-Check-Act Cycle

Like Deming, Juran also advanced the Quality movement in Japan. Juran's approach to quality management insists that products and services should have "fitness for use" for customers. In other words, the product or service should be dependable for what the user wants or needs to do. Juran developed a process to achieve "fitness for use" that analyzed the life of a product or service from its initial design to the point that the product or service reached the customer.

Juran also developed what is called the Juran Trilogy, which emphasizes Quality Improvement, Quality Planning, and Quality Control, as shown in Exhibit 1-2. In addition to this trilogy, Juran is known for his Ten Steps to Quality Improvement.

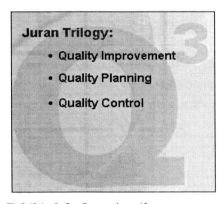

Exhibit 1-2: Juran's trilogy

Crosby served as the Vice President of Quality at ITT before starting the Crosby Quality College. Crosby's approach to quality focused on upper management, and he referred to quality as "conformance to requirements." Therefore, according to Crosby, any product that conformed to its design requirements was a high quality product. Using this reasoning, Crosby asserted that quality management could be applied to the production of any product or service, not just to high-end products and services.

Crosby supported the concept of zero defects and thought it could be achieved by building quality into work processes instead of relying on inspection when a product is completed. Crosby's approach to creating continuous improvement started with changing the attitudes of upper management and then applying a 14-point program that emphasized prevention over inspection.

Quality management and the previous quality efforts

Quality management is the result or outgrowth of previous quality efforts. Quality management takes the best aspects of quality circles, statistical process control, and other quality efforts and combines them together in a single approach. Quality management encompasses more than each of the previous individual quality efforts, and it puts each of the efforts into context and describes when to use them.

Do it!

A-1: The Quality movement

Exercise

1 Which individual in the following list led the quality management approaches given below: Deming; Juran; Crosby?

Conformance to requirements

Plan-Do-Check-Act Cycle

Ten Steps to Quality Improvement

Importance of incorporating quality into daily management

Explanation

Incorporating continuous quality improvement efforts on a daily basis can help an organization take full advantage of its human resources. An organization that establishes a quality management process and expects all of its members to work toward improvement every day will improve the quality of its products and services, which leads to increased market share, loyal customers, and satisfied employees.

Who should be involved in the daily management of quality?

Every employee in an organization should be involved in the daily management of quality. Allowing employees to participate in continuous improvement by measuring and controlling their work processes everyday helps them see their impact on the company and makes them feel valued and important.

Role of management in implementing quality

Management must lead the movement for continually improving quality. Managers should lead their employees by example, so that employees can see how a focus on quality benefits the company and customers. In addition, Deming states that because only management can change the system in which all employees work, most of the responsibility for quality improvement belongs to management.

Deming also asserts that workers find intrinsic motivation in a job well done. Therefore, management must overcome its preconceived notion that problems with quality are due to workers who do not perform their jobs correctly. For example, suppose you have hired the best employee possible for a particular job. If that employee begins work with low quality materials, no training, and inadequate equipment, he or she will probably not be able to produce products that are free of defects, which highlights the importance of management's role in ensuring quality.

Deming believes management must strive to continuously improve the systems employees work in, and it must replace the traditional notions of supervision and inspection with training and education. For example, suppose a new employee is making errors that cause product defects. If the mistakes are a result of insufficient training, management must determine why the employee has not been properly trained. A possible answer might be that not enough money has been budgeted for training, which is an issue management should investigate and change.

Another example of the importance of management's role in ensuring quality is shown in the following situation. Suppose the quality of a product is poor, and the source of the quality problem stems from poor components. Management needs to determine why the organization is receiving poor quality components. A possible answer might be that company policy wants buyers to purchase components from the lowest bidder. The resulting poor quality product indicates that management needs to change the policy in order to improve quality.

Do it! ## A-2: Quality in daily management

Exercises

1 Only the management is involved in the daily management of quality.

   A True

   B False

2 You are a manager in Icon International's production department. You got Tim transferred into your department one month ago because of his excellent performance in the previous department. However, he is now making errors that cause product defects. What could be the possible reasons for Tim's poor performance?

3 Select the choices that reflect management's role in implementing quality.

   A Management must lead by example.

   B Management must continually improve the systems in which employees work.

   C Management must implement strict quotas.

   D Management must provide extrinsic motivation for workers.

   E Management must replace inspection with education.

Processes for improvements in daily management

Explanation
In order to incorporate improvements into daily management, organizations must first standardize all work processes that create a desired output. By standardizing the processes, organizations can ensure that the desired output is being achieved company wide, which allows them to maintain the current level of performance. This standardization process is known as the SDCA cycle, which comprises the following steps: Standardize the process, Do it, Check it, and Act if further adjustment is needed, as shown in Exhibit 1-3.

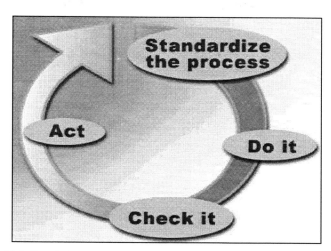

Exhibit 1-3: The SDCA cycle

The second step organizations should take is to strive for continuous improvement. Continuous improvement is necessary when output does not meet expectations and when customers' needs change. The PDCA cycle helps implement steps for continuous improvement. It consists of the following steps: Plan the process change, Do it, Check it, and Act if further adjustments are needed, as shown in Exhibit 1-4.

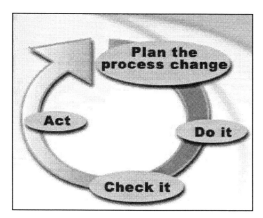

Exhibit 1-4: The PDCA cycle

The final step organizations need to take to incorporate improvements into daily management is to innovate. They should continually search for ways to increase the quality of their work processes. When new methods are found, they should be incorporated using the PDCA cycle.

Do it!

A-3: Incorporating improvements into daily management

Exercise

1 Identify and sequence the steps an organization should follow to incorporate improvements into daily management.

Strive for continuous
improvement

Innovate to increase the quality of
work processes

Conduct customer research

Standardize work processes

Use benchmarks and standards

Topic B: Processes

Explanation

Any of the work you do throughout the day is a *process*. Filing a report, preparing statements, designing a training course, writing a software program, and producing a part are all processes. Regardless of what work you do or where you complete it, your work is a process.

Process variation

Process variation is the fluctuation of process performance. Although some have considerably more than others, all processes have variation. For example, you don't arrive at work at exactly the same time everyday. The fluctuation in your arrival time shows the variation in your "drive to work" process. Other examples of variation include the time required to process insurance forms or the exact diameter of a drilled hole.

Although small amounts of variation in process performance might seem relatively harmless, variation is unwanted because it causes uncertainty. Uncertainty about process performance and outcomes inhibits your ability to manage the process. If you don't know what to expect from a process, you can't plan around the outcomes of the process.

Effects of variation

Variation ultimately leads to loss, which can occur in two ways. First, variation can cause customer dissatisfaction, which leads to fewer sales and possibly a decrease in customer loyalty. Second, loss can waste resources that are used for paying out warranties, scrapping work, redoing work, as well as analyzing, inspecting, and testing work.

Views on variation

Traditionally, variance has been viewed as acceptable as long as the products and services produced fell within customer requirements for satisfaction. In this view of variation, any point within the customer satisfaction specifications is said to be acceptable, and any point outside the specifications is unacceptable.

This view of variation assumes that no loss occurs from variation within the customer satisfaction specifications. Similarly, it assumes that all points outside the specifications incur the same amount of loss. This viewpoint is known as "goal post" thinking because it is analogous to kicking a field goal in football. Regardless of where the ball lands, if it is within the goal posts it is good; if it is outside the goal posts it is bad.

Another view of variation is needed because it is not realistic to assume that customer dissatisfaction never occurs inside the specifications or that all points outside the specifications result in the same level of dissatisfaction. Realistically, there is one point, usually in the middle of the specifications, that produces what the customer wants. At this point, no loss is incurred. Any point that varies from the desired point incurs loss. The farther points are from the desired point, the more loss they incur.

Do it!

B-1: Variation in processes

Exercises

1 Select the ways in which process variation leads to loss.

   A Shifts in consumer needs

   B Customer dissatisfaction

   C Market fluctuations

   D Wasted resources

   E Employee dissatisfaction

2 A few examples of processes (and possible variations) are:

   • Writing a report (errors)

   • Developing a product (high cycle time)

   • Delivering a product (not on time)

   • Budgeting (delay)

   • Invoicing (errors)

   List three more processes and variations you are familiar with and share them in the class.

Causes of variation

Explanation

There are two distinct causes of variation: common causes and special causes. Common causes of variation are inherent to the process. In other words, they are built into the process and are a normal part of how the process functions. Variations stemming from common causes will cause collected data to vary in a random manner.

Workers cannot be held responsible for this type of variation, and if the level of variation in a process is unacceptable, management must replace or fix the system in order to decrease the amount of variance. Some examples of how the system can be changed to eliminate common causes of variation include training operators to reduce the variation by standardizing the process performed, purchasing parts from only a single vendor to reduce the variation from vendor to vendor, and using a new tool, guide, template, or form to standardize the way the process is performed.

The second type of variance is a result of special causes. Examples of special causes include different raw materials, new procedures, or significant changes in temperature, as well as new or different operators, tools, or equipment. Special causes are not part of the process, and they often can be fixed by the people involved with the process. Special causes are usually easier to identify than common causes, and they cause collected data to vary in a nonrandom manner.

Although employees can usually remove special causes, management should create a policy that prevents the special cause from producing variance in the future. Occasionally, variance produced by special causes results in a positive outcome. In this situation, management should establish a policy that incorporates the special cause as an intentional part of the process.

Some frequent sources of variation

Poor management is a frequent source for variation resulting from both common and special causes. Quality management founders Juran and Deming assert that 85 percent of quality problems can be traced back to management.

There are a variety of reasons why management is responsible for many of the quality problems in an organization. One shortcoming is that management might not understand the impact of variation on quality, production time, and operational costs. As a result, management might not have developed an effective policy for achieving reduced variation.

Even organizations that recognize the impact of variation might not provide the leadership and resources needed to achieve variation reduction. For example, to achieve variation reduction, more time and energy must be applied to building quality into the process than is applied to "putting out fires."

Other frequent sources of variation include inadequate product, process, and component specifications. Frequently, these specifications are wrong, too vague to be helpful, or missing altogether. In addition to inadequate specifications, variance can result from poor manufacturing practices and inadequate supplier materials.

A final source of variation is operator error. Operator errors can be caused by a number of factors including poor instructions, training, processes, equipment, and materials. The root of operator errors can also be a design that is not easily manufactured or managerial beliefs that workers cannot or should not think for themselves.

Do it!

B-2: Causes of variation

Exercises

1 John, quality supervisor at Icon, has noticed variations in the workflow of the employees over the last two months. He has identified two causes of variation: purchasing parts from different vendors and significant changes in temperature. Classify these causes as common causes and special causes so that appropriate policies can be made.

2 Select the characteristics of common causes of variation.

   A   Can often be fixed by people involved with the process.

   B   Cause collected data to vary in a nonrandom manner.

   C   Cause collected data to vary in a random manner.

   D   Not an inherent part of a process.

   E   Are a normal part of how a process functions.

Unit summary: Fundamentals of quality management

Topic A   In this unit, you learned the concepts commonly associated with **quality management**, the **role of management** in implementing quality, and the steps an organization should follow to incorporate **improvements** into daily management.

Topic B   Finally, you learned the ways in which **variation** leads to loss, the characteristics of **common causes** of variation, and the frequent sources of variation.

Review questions

1 Determine which one of the following is a quality manager's goal.

   a To improve continuously by striving for a high degree of variation in work processes.

   b To maintain current level of performance by striving for a high degree of variation in work processes.

   c To improve continuously by finding ways to make processes work better.

   d To maintain current level of performance by using existing quality processes.

2 How would you deal with a situation in which an employee is making errors that cause product defects?

   a Determine whether or not the employee has been properly trained.

   b Focus all efforts on fixing the product defects.

   c Require the employee to go through the training process a second time.

   d Institute new training processes immediately.

3 Which of the following set of steps should you follow to ensure a constant level of performance?

   a Standardize the process, Do it, Check it, and Act if further adjustment is needed (SDCA).

   b Standardize the process, Do it, Check it, and Monitor it annually (SDCM).

   c Plan the process, Check it, and Act if further adjustment is needed (PCA).

   d Plan the process, Standardize the process, Do it, and Act if further adjustment is needed (PSDA).

4 Which is the final step in increasing the quality of your organization's work processes?

   a Focus on maintenance

   b Focus on innovation

   c Focus on increasing variation

   d Focus on increasing resources

5 Identify the definition of process variation.

   a Any rapid decrease in process performance

   b The process by which performance is regulated

   c The fluctuation of process performance

   d The steady increase of process performance

6 Determine how your customers would react after buying a defective product from your company.

   a They would just accept the situation and their loyalty to your company would remain constant.

   b They would eventually buy even more products from your company.

   c They would be less loyal to your company.

   d They would be even more loyal to your company to show their support for your products.

7 Determine where search for variations in your department would lead you most of the time.

   a To any equipment involved in the variation

   b The decisions you and other managers have made

   c To consumers who might not be using the product as intended

   d To all the employees in the department

8 Which of the following is a shortcoming that could be a reason for variation.

   a I haven't understood the true impact of variation on quality, time, and costs.

   b I haven't spent enough time reviewing company policies.

   c My management training has focused only on how to effectively manage variation within an organization.

   d I haven't been able to understand the role I play outside the organization.

9 Select the characteristics of common causes of variation.

    a Workers can't be held responsible for this type of variation

    b Can be individually identified and singled out for elimination

    c Management should create a policy to eliminate future occurrences

    d Management must replace or fix the system to decrease the variance

Unit 2

The costs of quality

Unit time: 30 minutes

Complete this unit, and you'll know how to:

A Identify the relationship between quality and cost, the benefits of establishing quality requirements, management's responsibilities for achieving conformance, and the costs of customer dissatisfaction.

Topic A: Relationship between quality and cost

Explanation

Before the quality revolution that began in the United States in the 1980s, quality was frequently viewed as a goal that came at a higher price for production. However, the reality is that poor quality is a result of the ineffective use of resources, including wasted material and labor. Therefore, improved quality means better use of resources and lower costs. In addition, better quality and lower costs help an organization compete in the market place, which allows that organization to not only stay in business but to grow as well.

Costs of quality

The costs of quality are commonly described using the following categories:

- *Internal failure costs*, which stem from defects found before a product reaches the customer. Some examples include repairing the defective products so they can be shipped to customers and the resources wasted in products that are beyond repair. These defects could be eliminated if no defects existed in the production process.

- *External failure costs*, which are a result of defects found by the customer. The costs incurred at this time include the cost of warranties, servicing the product, and costs associated with returned goods. Like internal failure costs, external failure costs can be eliminated by solving problems in the production process.

- *Appraisal costs*, which stem from resources needed to conduct inspections of raw materials, work-in-process materials, and end products. Appraisal costs can be reduced by developing plans that prevent defects in the raw and work-in-process materials, as well as the final products.

- *Prevention costs*, which are the expenses incurred from initiatives implemented to prevent defects in products, such as evaluations of suppliers, employee training, and other plans made for achieving quality.

Another way of looking at the costs of quality was popularized by Philip Crosby. He separates the costs into two components. The first is the *price of non-conformance* (PONC), which can be described as the cost of not doing things right the first time. The price of non-conformance includes the cost of rework and the cost of repairing products with warranties. According to Crosby, the price of non-conformance can represent 20 percent or more of the sales in manufacturing organizations and 35 percent of operating costs in service organizations.

Crosby's second component is the *price of conformance*, which can be described as the cost of doing things right the first time. The price of conformance (POC) includes the expenses of educating employees and inspecting products.

Do it!   **A-1:   Identifying the costs of quality**

Exercises

1 Select the choice that accurately describes a result of improved quality.

   A   Enhanced inspection efforts

   B   Increased time for production

   C   Better use of resources and lower costs

   D   Higher price for production

2 Consider the following activities that are undertaken as prevention costs: taking the car for regular maintenance, training new employees, listing 'to do items' every morning, preparing a meeting agenda, and undertaking preventive maintenance of equipment.

   List three more activities that can be undertaken as prevention costs in your organization.

3 Discuss how prevention can help in reducing the price of non-conformance (PONC).

4 The price of non-conformance (PONC) is what it costs to do things wrong. It is the cost of waste: wasted material, effort, and time. On the other hand, the price of conformance (POC) is what it costs to ensure that things are done right the first time and that processes conform. Classify the following costs into PONC or POC elements.

Costs related to:	PONC/POC	Costs related to:	PONC/POC
Invoice errors		Auditing	
Complaint handling		Procedure audit	
High receivables		Litigation	
High inventory		Downtime due to breakdown	
Scrap		Preventive maintenance	
Incoming inspection		Delay in dispatch of finished goods	
Software verifications		Product returns	
Training needs identification		Procedure audit	
Product testing (in process)		Rework	

Establishing quality requirements for products or services

Explanation

Establishing quality requirements for products and services defines what quality is. Without clear requirements, quality is often equated with "goodness," which is interpreted differently by every individual within an organization. Without requirements, organizations must rely on opinions and hunches about what constitutes quality work. When quality is defined as conformance to requirements, every individual understands what he or she must do to create quality products and services.

Establishing requirements up front also makes better use of an organization's resources. Employees can spend less time on rework, and managers can spend less time figuring out how to resolve quality issues in products and services that have already been produced.

Importance of meeting the established requirements every time

It is important to meet the established requirements every time because it reduces costs. Doing work right the first time is less time-consuming and expensive than redoing work. In addition, if the requirements have been properly established, meeting them every time ensures customer satisfaction.

Why are requirements more effective for quality control than appraisal?

Appraisal, which might also be known as inspection, testing, or checking, is not as effective as requirements because appraisals are completed after a product is complete. Appraisals separate the good final products from the bad final products. Requirements, on the other hand, build quality into a product, which means product defects are prevented.

Do it!

A-2: Quality requirements for products or services

Exercises

1 What are the advantages of maintaining first-time quality?

2 Select the benefits of establishing quality requirements for products and services.

   A   Incorporates frequently overlooked costs of customer dissatisfaction

   B   Allows managers to spend less time determining how to resolve quality issues

   C   Defines what quality is

   D   Allows for multiple interpretations of "goodness"

   E   Enables employees to spend less time on rework

   F   Helps individuals understand how to create quality products and services

The 1-10-100 rule

Explanation

The 1-10-100 rule was introduced by G.H. Loabovitz and Y.S. Chang. The purpose of the 1-10-100 rule is to demonstrate the costs of allowing quality problems.

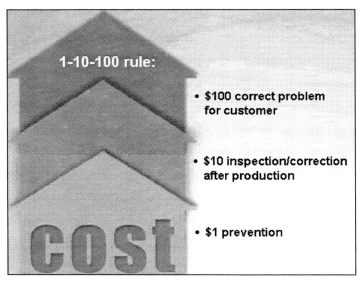

Exhibit 2-1: The 1-10-100 rule

The rule (as shown in Exhibit 2-1) states that for every one dollar an organization spends to prevent a quality problem it would have to spend 10 dollars to inspect and correct the mistake after the product was made, and it would have to spend 100 dollars to rectify the problem after it has reached the customer. Furthermore, many experts in the quality field believe that this rule underestimates the cost of defective products reaching the hands of customers. Some believe the correct number is closer to 500 or 1000.

Costs of customer dissatisfaction

When estimating their costs of quality, organizations frequently overlook certain costs that are caused by customer dissatisfaction. Although companies might measure the costs of repairing defective products, paying warranties, and returned products, they often fail to consider the costs of lost revenue and the effects of a bad reputation.

Management's responsibility for achieving conformance

Explanation

In his book *Quality Without Tears*, Crosby says that management has three basic responsibilities for helping employees do their work correctly the first time. The first is to establish the requirements that employees should meet. The second is to provide the resources employees need to achieve the requirements. The third is to continually encourage and assist employees as they work to meet the requirements. Keep in mind that employees will take requirements only as seriously as management takes them, so management must lead by example.

Conditions mistakenly viewed as the causes of poor quality

When management does not recognize the importance of its role in achieving quality, it often mistakenly views several conditions as the cause of poor quality. Those conditions include worker attitudes, product designs, and the quality of parts received from suppliers. In some cases, management simply accepts that only a certain level of quality can be achieved. When management resigns itself to the fact that a certain number of errors will always occur, it gives the entire company permission to consider that error rate as the definition of quality work.

Do it!

A-3: Management's responsibilities

Exercises

1 Select the responsibilities management has for achieving conformance.

    A   Provide the resources employees need to achieve the requirements.

    B   Determine whether worker attitudes or product designs are causing quality problems.

    C   Encourage and assist employees as they work to meet requirements.

    D   Accept that only a certain level of quality can be achieved.

    E   Establish the requirements that employees should meet.

2 Identify some of the conditions managers mistakenly consider to be causes of poor quality?

Unit summary: The costs of quality

Topic A

In this unit, you learned about the relationship between **quality and cost**. Then you learned about the importance of achieving quality requirements for products or services, as well as the costs of **customer dissatisfaction**. You also learned that the **1-10-100** rule shows how costly it can be not to build quality into processes. Finally, you learned about management's responsibilities in achieving conformance.

Review questions

For all the following questions, assume that you are the Quality Control Manager of a company called MCorp.

1 MCorp is ready to release a new microchip in the open market. Before the release, however, a defect is found. What type of cost will it be to fix the defect and get the microchip released?

    a Prevention costs

    b Internal failure costs

    c External failure costs

    d Appraisal costs

2 In your efforts to make sure no defective products reach your customers, you implement more inspections to assure the quality of your products in all stages of development. How would you classify the costs of these inspections?

    a Contracted costs

    b Prevention costs

    c Appraisal costs

    d Implementation costs

3 To prevent defective microchips from reaching the open market, you need to turn your attention to issues such as suppliers and employee training procedures. Determine how would you classify the costs of dealing with these issues.

    a Production costs

    b Prevention costs

    c Analysis costs

    d Initiative costs

4 Identify Crosby's terms for the two components of costs associated with quality.

   a Price of conformance, price of non-conformance

   b Cost of correspondence, cost of non-correspondence

   c Price of development, price of production

   d Price of regulation, price of deregulation

5 Identify the rule-of-thumb regarding how much more it costs an organization to fix problems after they reach customers.

   a The 5-10-100 rule

   b The 1-10-100 rule

   c The 1-50-500 rule

   d The 10-50-100 rule

6 If your employees know what their requirements are and they have the motivation required to do the job, but they still are not having much success, what can you do to help them?

   a Let employees work through problems on their own.

   b Try to motivate employees by constantly encouraging them.

   c Reiterate employee requirements, so they all know exactly what is expected of them.

   d Make sure they have the resources they need to achieve the requirements.

7 As a manager, your attitude toward quality will ultimately reflect on your employees and, by extension, MCorp. Determine what quality standard you need to set for your organization.

   a Make your product as close to error-free as possible.

   b A certain level of error is unavoidable.

   c The only acceptable goal is error-free products.

   d Errors are a part of every process and should be viewed as educational opportunities.

8 As a manager, it is your job not to overlook any costs associated with customer dissatisfaction, such as repairing defective products or paying warranties, but costs do get overlooked. Which of the following is an example of a cost of customer dissatisfaction that is often overlooked?

   a The revenue generated by the production equipment

   b The revenue from returned products

   c The effect of a bad reputation

   d The cost of employees dedicated to customer service

U n i t 3

Customer orientation

Unit time: 45 minutes

Complete this unit, and you'll know how to:

A Identify the characteristics of and steps toward being customer-oriented, as well as approaches to customer research.

B Identify the benefits of a customer-oriented organization.

Topic A: Understanding customer orientation

Explanation

Customer orientation is an organizational mindset in which meeting the needs of the customer becomes an organization's focus. Customer orientation is an important aspect of quality management because it ensures customer satisfaction by integrating the customer's needs into strategic planning, product development, and product delivery. There are three components that comprise customer orientation: awareness of the market, communication of market intelligence to the entire organization, and initiatives to make use of the market intelligence.

Customers

Customers are any individuals or groups of individuals to whom you provide products or services. It is important to consider that customers can be internal or external. Satisfying internal customers is part of the process of satisfying external customers. Knowing who your internal customers are allows you to get feedback on your performance, determine what is most important to your customers, and ultimately measure how well you are doing. When all of the internal supplier and customer relationships are functioning well, the external customer is more likely to be satisfied.

Do it!

A-1: Importance of customer orientation

Exercises

1   If your company delivers quality products and services to external customers, why are internal customers important?

2   Select the group of people whose opinion about the level of satisfaction provided by a product or service is most important.

   A   Management

   B   Investors

   C   Customers

   D   Employees

3 With respect to the work you do (products or services), identify your internal and external customers.

Work I do	Internal customers	External customers

Customer-oriented organizations

Explanation

Customer-oriented organizations do the following things:

- Maintain ongoing communication with the customer base.
- Empower employees to take actions needed to satisfy customers.
- Possess commitment from upper management.
- Include all employees in the effort to satisfy customers.
- Recognize employees for customer service success.

Importance of customer orientation

Organizations need to be customer-oriented because unless they clearly understand their customers' needs, they cannot meet them. It is critical to understand that customers, not management, determine the level of satisfaction provided by a product or service. Service is not good, or even satisfactory, unless customers say it is. Therefore, the perception management has of the quality of service their organization provides is irrelevant unless it coincides with customers' viewpoints.

Primary pitfall of not being customer-oriented

Frequently, when organizations are not focused on benefiting the customer, they waste resources implementing changes that are not important to the customer. New products or improvements to existing products that do not reflect customers' expectations and needs are not beneficial, and the resources used to create them are wasted. Therefore, organizations need to take steps to discover what changes will make an actual difference to customers.

Transition to customer orientation

Becoming customer-orientated is not a transition that can occur overnight. The process must be carefully planned. To make the transition successfully, organizations must take actions to shift the thinking of all employees within the organization. There are two high-level steps to this transition:

1 The first step in the process for becoming customer-oriented is for management to commit to the transition. Employees might initially resist adopting a customer orientation because it will change the way they perform their jobs. Therefore, management needs to be firm and ready to lead employees through the change. Management's role must be to support and guide employees to serve customers as well as possible. It is management's responsibility to make sure that every action taken reflects commitment to the customer. This goal can be accomplished by increasing employees' ability to create exceptional products and give exceptional service. Keep in mind that employees are management's internal customers, and the way management serves its employees provides an example for the way the employees should serve their customers.

2 The second and final step is actually a series of ongoing actions that must be taken to maintain customer orientation:

- Conduct customer research.
- Train and empower employees.
- Use benchmarks and standards.
- Provide employees with necessary resources.
- Recognize successes.

Conduct customer research

Although many organizations might conduct *customer research*, many of them do not do so on a continual basis. To understand customers' changing needs and wants, the organization must gather feedback regularly. This will ensure that products and services are what customers want, instead of what the organization thinks they want.

Train and empower employees

A customer-oriented organization must train its employees in teamwork and problem-solving skills. Doing so enables employees to adopt the collaborative attitude necessary for quality management. Many employees might also need training in customer research techniques.

Employees also need to be empowered in their positions to provide quality service. *Empowerment* equips employees to serve customers better by giving them some flexibility in their interactions. Even talented employees can be stifled in their ability to meet customers' needs if they have to adhere to a strict set of rules that does not allow them the freedom to treat every customer as an individual. In addition, empowered employees can make decisions and complete tasks that once required the assistance of a manager.

Use benchmarks and standards

Based on what an organization learns through customer research, it should establish benchmarks and standards by which to gauge the quality of its work. *Benchmarking* involves learning how other companies perform specific processes, so an organization can gain ideas for improving or overhauling the way it performs the process.

Benchmarking also helps an organization compare its performance to that of its competitors, so it does not lose customers. *Standards*, which can be set by management, are helpful when benchmarks are not available. Standards help organizations set guidelines for performing specific tasks.

Provide employees with necessary resources

For employees to provide high-quality products and services to their customers, they need certain resources. Organizations that want to develop a customer orientation should supply their employees with resources that can help them perform at the desired level. For example, in some cases, customer satisfaction might depend on an organization investing in new high-tech equipment.

However, organizations should not overlook the importance of low-tech solutions. Often, a knowledgeable and sincere human being is the most important element of service to a customer. For example, think about the quality of service you received the last time you returned an item to a department store. The quality of service probably depended on whether the employee had the necessary resources to provide you with good service.

Recognize successes

As employees work to adopt a customer orientation, management should be sure to provide appropriate and meaningful recognition along the way. Recognizing employees for their efforts helps motivate them to continue making quality improvements. In addition, this recognition is noticed by others and encourages them to participate in a similar manner.

Do it!

A-2: Becoming customer-oriented

Multiple-choice questions

1 Select the choice that describes management's role in the first step in the process of becoming customer-oriented.

   A A supervisory position in which management monitors employees' ability to meet customers' needs.

   B A support position in which management provides guidance to employees.

   C A secondary position in which management allows employees space to make the transition.

   D An authoritative position in which management demands the best performance from all employees.

2 Select the ongoing actions management should take to maintain customer orientation.

   A Investigate special causes of variation.

   B Ask for more commitment from employees.

   C Provide employees with necessary resources.

   D Eliminate sources of variation.

   E Use benchmarks and standards.

   F Train and empower employees.

   G Recognize successes.

   H Conduct customer research.

Conducting customer research

Explanation

In order to discover what customers want, organizations must develop a system that allows them to regularly gather customer research. Organizations can use any of the following approaches:

- Focus groups
- Interviews
- Questionnaires
- Comment cards

Focus groups

Focus groups, which consist of five to ten customers, are a formal means of gathering information. The customers are asked to give feedback about product samples. A focus group (illustrated in Exhibit 3-1) is most effective when its members are representative of the customer base, so a company receives information about how to satisfy as many customers as possible.

Exhibit 3-1: Focus group

Interviews

Interviews are one-on-one discussions with a customer. Surveys might be completed in person or over the telephone. Informal interviews can be as simple as a member of management sitting down with a customer to discuss what the organization can do to better meet the customer's needs. The interview could even be a follow-up call used to check on a customer's satisfaction with a product or service. During follow-up calls, employees can obtain valuable feedback about a customer's expectations and needs, as well as any problems he or she has experienced.

Questionnaires

Questionnaires are helpful when customers are not close enough to allow for focus groups or interviews. Questionnaires (illustrated in Exhibit 3-2) should be used to try to obtain the same information as an interview. It is important that questionnaires be sent to a random group of people so the feedback is representative of the entire customer base.

Exhibit 3-2: A sample questionnaire

Comment cards

Comment cards (illustrated in Exhibit 3-3) can be used to collect specific information about customer satisfaction. They can be set out in convenient places in stores. After the comment cards have been returned, someone should contact any dissatisfied customers to ask what changes they might want.

Exhibit 3-3: A sample comment card

Do it!

A-3: Conducting customer research

Group discussion

1 Which approach, in your opinion, best provides in-depth information about customer satisfaction?

   A Focus group

   B Interview

   C Questionnaire

   D Comment card

Topic B: Benefits of customer orientation

Explanation

Orienting an organization's goals around customers is profitable. When an organization focuses on meeting the wants and needs of its customers, the organization can create products and services that not only satisfy customers but also help develop loyal customers.

More than satisfied customers

Although satisfying customers is important, it might not be enough to keep customers coming back in the future. In fact, many customers who say they are satisfied with a company's services might switch to a competitor without hesitation. Studies show that as many as 65 to 85 percent of customers who say they are satisfied would be willing to purchase services from another company. Therefore, satisfying customers is the lowest level of acceptable service, as shown in Exhibit 3-4.

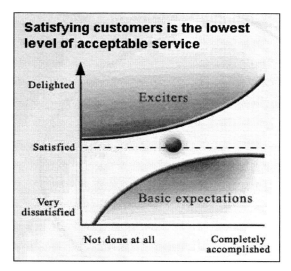

Exhibit 3-4: Satisfying customers

If an organization wants to create loyal customers, it must not only satisfy customers' needs but also exceed their expectations (as shown in Exhibit 3-5). An organization can exceed customers' expectations by providing them with unexpected surprises or features, often referred to as *customer exciters*. Customer exciters are important because they can convert satisfied customers into return customers who tell others about their positive experience.

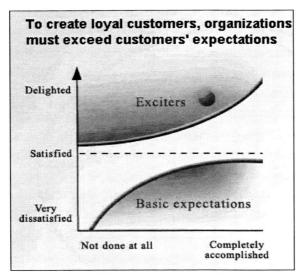

Exhibit 3-5: Exceeding customers' expectations

Achieving customer loyalty

To achieve *customer loyalty*, an organization must demonstrate a long-term commitment to its customers. The organization must provide consistently good service, it must provide something more than the competition provides, and it must build a relationship with the customers over time.

Some companies attempt to use a quick fix when trying to increase customer loyalty. For example, they might offer a free, temporary service or a discount card. Although these offers might cause a temporary increase in business, they will not develop customer loyalty. To do so, an organization must always meet customers' basic expectations, as well as frequently exceed them. Therefore, every aspect of an organization must be built to serve the customer effectively, requiring careful planning and implementation of a long-term strategy.

Do it!

B-1: Satisfying customers

Exercises

1 Discuss why an organization must not only satisfy customers' needs, but also exceed them, in order to develop customer loyalty.

2 Select the percentage of satisfied customers who would still be willing to purchase services from another company.

   A 85 to 95 percent

   B 5 to 10 percent

   C 65 to 85 percent

   D 20 to 30 percent

Benefits of loyal customers

Explanation

Loyal customers can provide several financial benefits for companies:

- Loyal customers increase their spending.
- Loyal customers talk about service.
- Loyal customers reduce costs.

Increased spending

Loyal customers are profitable because their spending usually accelerates over time. If an organization offers a variety of products and services, there is great potential for spending growth. Customers will usually purchase more goods and services from an organization if they are satisfied with their initial purchases.

For example, suppose a customer takes his or her car to a service station for an oil change. If the customer is happy, he or she might return when the car needs other services. If the customer remains happy, he or she might rely on that service station for all repairs, which might include other vehicles.

Loyal customers talk about service

Because as much as 50 percent of purchases made are based on word-of-mouth advertising, it is critical for an organization to provide service that customers want to talk about. Keep in mind that customers are more likely to talk about a bad experience than a good experience. Therefore, an organization must provide products and services that make customers want to spread positive messages.

The free advertising loyal customers provide can reduce the amount of money needed for advertising. Moreover, people typically consider word-of-mouth advertising to be more truthful than advertisements created by a company.

Reduced costs

Creating loyal customers can reduce costs in several ways. One way is to greatly reduce the need to acquire new customers, because loyal customers tell others about their positive experiences. Acquiring new customers can be as much as six times more expensive than maintaining the happiness of current customers.

Loyal customers also reduce costs because they are familiar with the organization and services it provides, frequently needing less assistance. Loyal customers can increase profits because they might be willing to pay slightly more for service from an organization with whom they have established a valued relationship.

Do it!   **B-2:   Financial incentives for developing loyal customers**

Multiple-choice question

1 Select the financial incentives for developing loyal customers.

    A   Loyal customers have unchanging expectations.

    B   Loyal customers increase their spending.

    C   Loyal customers accept "exciters" over reliability.

    D   Loyal customers talk about service.

    E   Loyal customers reduce costs.

Unit summary: Customer orientation

Topic A

In this unit, you learned about the characteristics of a **customer-oriented organization**. You learned that the first step toward becoming customer-oriented is a **commitment from management**, and that there are a series of actions management must take after that to remain customer-oriented. You also learned several approaches to conducting **customer research**.

Topic B

Then you learned some of the benefits of developing a customer orientation. You saw that satisfying customers is necessary but not sufficient. Finally, you learned about the **financial incentives** of developing **loyal customers**.

Review questions

Recent customer surveys have shown that Icon has become less customer-friendly in the past year. Management has noted this trend and is acting to reverse it by appointing several Customer Service managers to reorient the company toward customer satisfaction. As the Quality Assurance Directors for Icon, the Customer Service managers responsible for the transition, Bernard Chan and Caroline Harris, have requested you to join them in a meeting. The agenda is to plan the steps for the transition, discuss possible methods to conduct customer research, and discuss the benefits of increasing customer satisfaction.

Objectives:

- Identify the characteristics of a customer-oriented organization.
- Identify the primary pitfall of not being customer-oriented.
- Identify the steps to become customer-oriented.
- Identify the ongoing steps management must take to maintain customer orientation.
- Identify the financial incentives for developing loyal customers.

Bernard starts the session by commenting on the optimism felt both by the company and the customers for the transition to increased customer satisfaction. Caroline agrees and adds that it is crucial for a customer-oriented organization to maintain constant communication with customers. She also points out that it is critical for the organization to empower its employees to take actions to satisfy customers.

Bernard observes that most organizations lose track of the objectives and invest time and resources on areas unimportant to customers. The first step should be total commitment of the management to the transition. Caroline says that apart from commitment by management, Icon needs to ensure that it understands customer needs by conducting constant research into customer satisfaction. If the employees are attuned to meeting customer needs and are empowered to take actions in this direction, the organization can maintain a loyal customer base. Moreover, employees must be given all the resources they want to maintain a high level of quality. This also includes appreciation and recognition from the management as encouragement for good work.

Bernard cites the case of a competitor who was very focused on customer satisfaction initially. But as the priorities shifted to higher profits, the quality of the products fell, and so did the customer base. Therefore, it is important to establish benchmarks and quality standards to ensure that quality is maintained at all times.

Caroline asks Bernard about the primary advantages of maintaining customer loyalty. Bernard replies that increased customer loyalty reduces costs in the long run as they need less assistance. Also, word-of-mouth referrals help reduce advertising costs and bring in new customers. He also adds that apart from reducing costs, loyal customers also contribute to the revenue of an organization as their spending accelerates over time.

Based on this discussion and the points collected, Bernard and Caroline feel that they can create a plan to kick off the transition to a more customer-oriented culture at Icon.

1 A customer-oriented organization (select all that apply):

   a Maintains constant communication with its customers.

   b Empowers employees to meet customer expectations.

   c Collaborates with other companies to offer the best product to customers.

   d Benchmarks products and services to offer the highest quality to customers.

   e Makes employees work in isolation from management.

   f Understands customer needs by conducting customer satisfaction research.

2 The primary disadvantage of not being customer-oriented is:

   a The quality of products and services suffers a drop.

   b The customer base is eroded.

   c Fewer customers send feedback.

   d The price of products and services has to be decreased.

3 List the steps involved in management ensuring that an organization becomes customer-oriented.

Unit 4

Understanding current performance

Unit time: 60 minutes

Complete this unit, and you'll know how to:

A Identify types of flow charts and create and analyze a flow chart.

B Create and analyze a check sheet.

C Create and interpret a histogram.

D Create and interpret a run chart.

E Identify characteristics of a control chart.

Topic A: Flow charts

Explanation

Flow charts, or *process flow diagrams*, are used to understand a process by documenting its steps. Understanding a process is essential for quality improvement because you must understand a process before you can control it. By documenting the entire process, flow charts can help teams identify areas in the process in which improvements can be made.

Benefits

Creating a flow chart of a process provides many benefits:

- **Clearly displays the process.** A flow chart can help anyone understand a process. This understanding is important when training new employees because they will be able to see immediately how they fit into the process. In addition, a completed flow chart helps all employees see the process in the same way.

- **Shows variance in work performance.** While creating a flow chart, a team might discover that each individual might complete a specific piece of work differently. When variances are discovered, the team should decide how the work should be performed and document the process to be followed by all employees in the future. Another type of variance occurs when all employees are completing work in a manner that differs from what was planned. In this situation, the process the employees actually use should be documented, and changes can be made if necessary. It is important to understand that documenting processes inaccurately will inhibit a team's ability to improve the process.

- **Increases employees' understanding.** Creating a flow chart helps show team members the interrelationships and dependencies that exist among different parts of the process, as well as among different individuals, teams, or departments. This knowledge shows team members how they fit into the process as a whole, teaching them about parts of the process in which they are not directly involved. This thorough understanding of a process can help employees improve communication among teams and departments.

- **Gives ownership to employees.** When employees clearly understand the process in which they work, they can take more ownership in ensuring that it is completed correctly. In addition, when employees understand how the work they perform influences others, they might be able to identify how they can do their work in a way that will decrease the workload of employees down the line.

- **Facilitates analysis of changes.** When a process is thoroughly documented in a flow chart, a team can clearly see how proposed changes will affect the process. This knowledge enables a team to adjust the proposed changes to eliminate problems during implementation.

Do it!

A-1: Benefits of using flow charts

Multiple-choice question

1 Select the benefits of flow charts.

  A They show variances in work performance.

  B They graphically display the variation in a data set.

  C They provide a running record of a process.

  D They give ownership to employees.

  E They clearly display processes.

Flow chart symbols

Explanation

Although specialized symbols exist for displaying information in flow charts, a simple system is all that is needed. Flow charts can be created using four symbols. An *activity*, displayed as a rectangle, can be used to represent each of the steps in a process. A *decision point*, displayed as a diamond, represents where decisions must be made before the process can continue. The paths proceeding from these points should be labeled "Yes" and "No." Arrows should be used to display the direction of flow of the process, and the start and stop points of the process can be displayed as ovals. "Start" and "Stop" should be written in the appropriate ovals. Exhibit 4-1 shows the four basic flow chart symbols, and Exhibit 4-2 shows a sample flow chart.

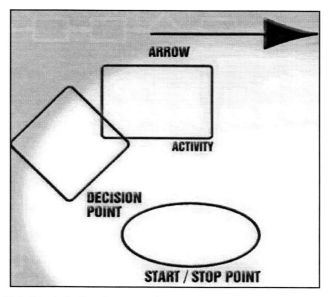

Exhibit 4-1: Symbols used in a flow chart

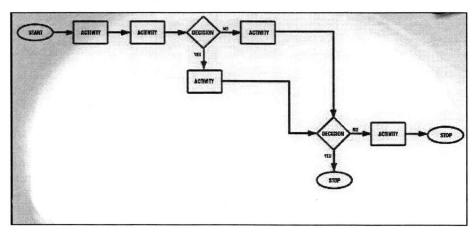

Exhibit 4-2: A sample flow chart

Do it!

A-2: Using flow chart symbols

Exercise
1 Which shape from the following list is used to describe each flow chart event given below: oval; small circle; diamond; large circle, rectangle, arrow? A decision point An activity The direction of flow A start point

Other types of flow charts

Explanation

In addition to the standard flow chart that depicts the activities and decisions that form a process, there are two other types of flow charts that can be helpful for analyzing a process. One type is the *functional flow chart*, which displays who is responsible for each activity and decision in the process. On a functional flow chart, horizontal lines drawn across the page are used to show the separation of responsibilities, as shown in Exhibit 4-3.

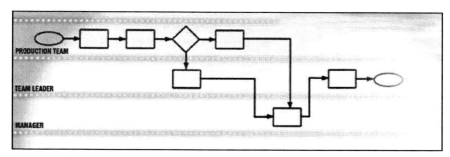

Exhibit 4-3: A sample functional flow chart

Each horizontal section represents a different individual, team, or department. These horizontal sections are sometimes called "swim lanes" because they look like the lanes competitive swimmers use in a race. The process is then added to the page, usually shown flowing left to right. The activities and decisions for which each group is responsible should be drawn in the appropriate horizontal section.

Another variation is the *layout flow chart*, also knows as the *geographic flow chart*, as shown in Exhibit 4-4. This type is used to show the flow of products, paperwork, and other materials. The chart should show a layout of a work area, including equipment, file cabinets, storage, and work stations. Then, arrows can be added to show how paperwork and other materials are passed through the area.

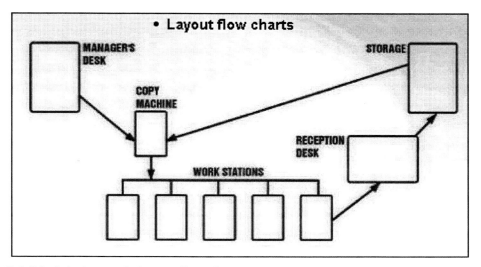

Exhibit 4-4: A sample layout flow chart

Do it!

A-3:   Using a functional flow chart

Multiple-choice question

1 Select the diagram that represents a functional flow chart.

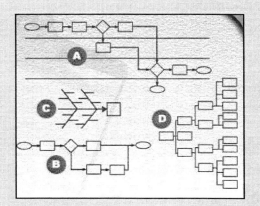

  A   Chart A

  B   Chart B

  C   Chart C

  D   Chart D

Topic B: Check sheets

Explanation

Check sheets are used to record the frequency of occurrence of various events. The format of the check sheet facilitates the counting of such data.

Creating check sheets

There are five steps you should follow to create a check sheet.

1 **Decide which data should be collected.** Determine for which events it is important to know the frequency of occurrence. Some events for which you might want to collect data include the number of mistakes in press releases, products damaged in shipping, or phone calls received.

2 **Identify possible categories in which to sort the event occurrences.** For example, if you were recording the number of telephone calls received from customers, you might want to know whether the calls were inquiries about products and services, complaints about products and services, or questions about billing.

3 **Determine the period of time over which the event occurrence should be measured.** The time frame will depend upon how often the event usually occurs. For an event that occurs every fifteen minutes, it might be necessary to collect data for a day. However, if an event usually occurs weekly, it might be necessary to record its occurrence over several months.

4 **Create the form.** Record the time period across the top of the page and record the categories down the left side.

5 **Record the data.** For each occurrence, place a tick mark in the appropriate category row and time column.

Do it!

B-1: Creating a check sheet

Exercises

1 Select the choice that best completes the sentence.

When there is a problem with the check sheet _____, there might be confusion about where to record events.

   A time period

   B title

   C design

   D operator

2 Avenue Electronics is a commercially successful TV manufacturing company. The company manufactures attractive and competitively priced TV models. However, the management found that sales of Model 528C were declining. Upon investigation, they found that a number of sets come back for repair within the warranty period. A corrective action team (CAT) was constituted to determine and eliminate the causes of the problem. Solving the problem would reduce the warranty cost and increase the reliability of the Model 528C.

The CAT found that integrated circuits, CRT, capacitors, resistors, transformers, and switches are mostly replaced. Jim Cassalla, a member of the CAT, decided to design a check sheet and record the data of the replaced parts for a period of three months. The check sheet made by him is as follows:

CHECK SHEET

Avenue Electronics: Component replacement within warranty period
Data gathered by: Jim Cassella
Model: 528C
Period: 1st March 2002 to 31st May 2002

Parts replaced	March 2002	April 2002	May 2002	Total
Switches	𝍏𝍏I	𝍏𝍏II	𝍏𝍏III	21
Capacitors	𝍏𝍏 𝍏𝍏 II	𝍏𝍏 𝍏𝍏𝍏𝍏	𝍏𝍏 𝍏𝍏𝍏𝍏II	44
Transformers	I	II	I	4
CRT	I		I	2
Integrated circuit	III	IIII	𝍏𝍏	12
Resistors	II	III	I	6
Total	25	31	33	89

Discuss the components of the check sheet and what defects Avenue Electronics should focus on first.

Location check sheet

Explanation

A variation can be made to the standard check sheet to create the *location check sheet*. The location check sheet can be used to record where an event occurred. For example, when measuring damage to shipped products, it would be important to know where the damage is occurring. Location check sheets can be created by drawing a picture of the area in which the event is going to occur. Then, an X can be marked on the diagram to identify the location of each occurrence.

Data collection pitfalls

When collecting data on a check sheet, it is critical that the information be recorded accurately. There are several pitfalls that can interfere with the collection of accurate data:

- **Poor design.** Be sure the categories are specific so that there are no uncertainties about where events should be recorded.

- **The specified time period.** Someone must be available to record data during the specified time.

- **Perceptions of the person recording.** Be sure the perceptions of the person recording the data do not interfere with accurate collection. The person must be familiar with events, so he or she can properly categorize them. He or she should also understand the importance of accurate information. Because some employees might be tempted to adjust data that shows ineffectiveness, it is important to emphasize that the process is being evaluated, not the employees themselves.

Topic C: Histograms

Explanation

Histograms are a specific type of bar chart that shows a graphic representation of the variation in a set of data, as shown in Exhibit 4-5. Using histograms to display the data can help identify patterns in the variation that would be difficult to see if the data were displayed in a table.

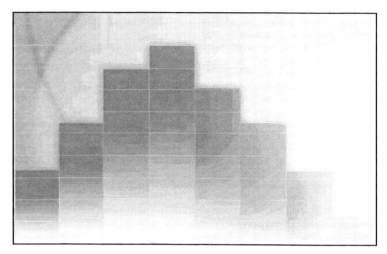

Exhibit 4-5: A sample histogram

Creating a histogram

There are seven steps in the process for creating a histogram:

1 **Gather data.**

2 **Determine the classes into which the measurements can be separated.** It might be helpful to think about the classes as buckets into which you can sort the data. A general rule for determining the number of classes needed is to find the square root of the number of data points collected. For example, suppose you had collected 37 data points. Because the square root of 37 is a little more than six, you would probably use six classes. Using the appropriate number of classes is important for proper analysis.

3 **Determine the width of each class.** The width means which numbers each bucket will hold. A general rule for determining class width is to divide the range of the data points by the number of classes needed (the range is the difference between the smallest data point from the largest).

   For example, suppose the smallest of the previously mentioned 37 data points is three and the largest is 75. In this case, the range is 72. The class width would be 72 divided by 6 (the number of classes), or 12. However, you could choose to round the class width to 10 or 15 for convenience.

4 **Define the classes.** When defining the classes, you should be sure that none of them overlap. The first class should begin with the smallest data point. For the 37 data points with a range of 72 and using a class width of 12, the classes would be three to 14, 15 to 26, 27 to 38, 39 to 50, 51 to 62, and 63 to 75.

5   **Determine the number of occurrences within each class.** This step requires sorting the collected data points into the appropriate classes. For example, you would count how many times the data collected from your process fell between three and 14, including both three and 14, and repeat this action for the remaining classes.

6   **Create the chart.** Label the horizontal axis with the classes. The vertical axis shows the number of occurrences, or the number of data points in each class. Label this axis with a scale that is appropriate for the data you have collected. You can determine the scale by identifying which class has the greatest number of data points.

For example, suppose the 27 to 38 class contains eight data points and that all the other classes contain fewer data points. In this case, a scale of zero to eight would be appropriate for the vertical axis.

7   **Draw the vertical bars for each class.** The height of each bar represents the number of data point occurrences in each class.

Do it!

C-1:   Creating a histogram

Exercises

1   Select the guideline for determining the number of classes for a histogram.

A   Find the square root of the class width.

B   Find the square root of the largest data point.

C   Find the square root of the number of data points collected.

D   Find the square root of the range of the data points collected.

2   Select the guideline for determining the class width for a histogram.

A   Divide the range of the data points by the largest data point.

B   Divide the largest data point by the range of the data points.

C   Divide the range of the data points by the number of classes.

D   Divide the number of classes needed by the range of the data points.

3   The last two steps in the process for creating a histogram are to create the chart and draw the bars. Sequence the first five steps of the process.

Determine class width.

Sort classes according to occurrence.

Determine occurrences per class.

Determine the number of classes.

Define the classes.

Gather data.

4 Histograms represent variation. Consider the following examples of variations that can be depicted and analyzed through histograms: the transaction time of tellers in a bank, time required to reach the office, number of minutes required to service a customer in a restaurant, time taken to resolve customer complaints, and time taken to prepare an invoice.

List a few examples of variations from your organization that can be depicted and analyzed through histograms.

Interpreting histograms

Explanation

After you have created a histogram, you need to analyze the variance it displays by observing the shape of the histogram. A small amount of variation is represented by a relatively small number of tall bars, while a large amount of variation is represented by a relatively large number of short bars, as shown in Exhibit 4-6.

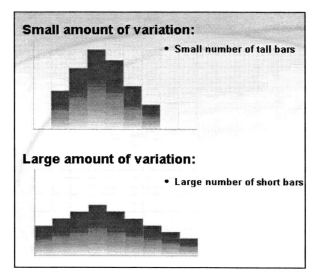

Exhibit 4-6: Variations in histograms

In other words, a tall and thin histogram would show little variation while a short and wide histogram would show a larger amount of variation.

Histograms commonly appear as a symmetrical shape with a single peak in the middle. This shape is also known as the *bell curve* (as shown in Exhibit 4-7). When observing a histogram shaped like a bell curve, you know that most of the data points lie in the middle. You also can see where the high and low data point extremes are located. Other shapes you might see include histograms with two humps or with a tail on either side of the peak. A tail is depicted by data that gradually trails off to either the left or right.

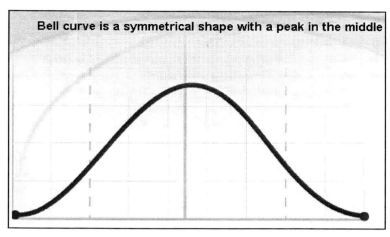

Exhibit 4-7: The bell curve

In addition to the shape of a histogram, the location of the data is also important. By comparing the location and width of a histogram to customers' requirements, you can determine whether a process will satisfy customers. A histogram shows you the range of existing performance, which can be compared to the range of acceptable performance needed to meet customer requirements, as shown in Exhibit 4-8. Any data points outside of the range of acceptable performance represent defects. This information tells you where your process is not performing well and needs improvement.

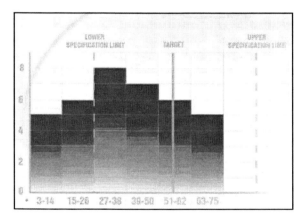

Exhibit 4-8: Histogram showing range of acceptable performance

Pitfall of histograms

Histograms do not show the time sequence in which the data was collected, so patterns could be present that are not displayed in the histogram. Therefore, you should use other methods of analysis, such as a run chart, in conjunction with the histogram to ensure you are not missing valuable information.

Do it!

C-2: Interpreting a histogram

Multiple-choice questions

1 The histograms in the following figure represent different processes that could be used to accomplish the same task. Since it is important to use processes with minimal variation, select the histogram that displays the least amount of variation.

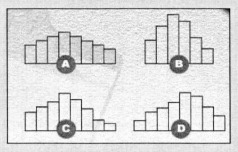

  A   Histogram A

  B   Histogram B

  C   Histogram C

  D   Histogram D

2 Select the histogram that displays the process that is in need of the most improvement.

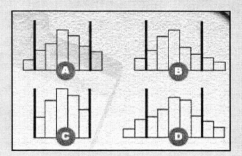

  A   Histogram A

  B   Histogram B

  C   Histogram C

  D   Histogram D

Topic D: Run charts

Explanation

A *run chart* is used to display the variation of a process characteristic over time.

Creating run charts

There are four steps you should follow to create a run chart:

1 **Choose a characteristic to analyze.** You might look at how many days it takes to get required signatures on a document, the number of hours of overtime worked, or the diameter of holes drilled in a part. Select carefully because analyzing the wrong characteristic might waste time or lead to improvement efforts that do not create the desired results.

2 **Determine the frequency of data collection.** The frequency will depend on the nature of the characteristic, but keep in mind that an unpredictable characteristic should be measured more often than a predictable one. For example, suppose you are measuring the diameters of drilled holes. If the holes are created by an accurate machine, you would not need to collect data as often as you would if the holes were produced by a manual, highly unpredictable process.

3 **Collect the data.**

4 **Create the chart and plot the data.** Label the horizontal axis with the time-order sequence, and label the vertical axis with an appropriate scale for the characteristic being measured, such as inches, minutes, or errors. Plot the points for the measurement of the characteristic at each time it was measured, and then connect the points.

Do it!

D-1:   Creating a run chart

Multiple-choice question

1 Identify and sequence the steps to create a run chart.

Draw the bars.

Collect the data.

Choose characteristic.

Choose frequency of data collection.

Create chart and plot data.

Collect data about both variables.

Interpreting run charts

Explanation

Similar to histograms, run charts show variation in a process. But, where a histogram shows a snapshot of a process, a run chart is more like a movie because it shows the performance of a process over time. Therefore, as you analyze run charts, you can see when a process is performing well, when it is performing poorly, and whether there are any patterns in the data.

Most of the time, data on a run chart appears to fluctuate randomly due to common cause variation. If a recognizable pattern is visible, something unusual is happening in the process. In this situation, you should investigate the process for special causes that are likely the source of the pattern.

Patterns common on run charts

Some patterns that commonly occur on run charts include cycles, mixtures, trends, and shifts, as shown in Exhibit 4-9.

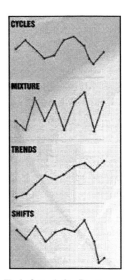

Exhibit 4-9: Patterns on run charts

Cycles appear as periodic waves of high and low points that repeat. Usually there are several data points between the high and low points. Mixtures are similar to cycles, but there are few or no data points between the high and low points. Trends show a series of points that steadily increase or decline. Shifts display a sudden shift from a prolonged series of high points to a prolonged series of low points, or vice versa.

When analyzing run chart patterns, be sure not to overemphasize every fluctuation in the data. Some fluctuation is always present and should not be interpreted as an indication of a problem.

Do it!

D-2:   Interpreting a run chart

Exercise

1 If a pattern is visible on a run chart, you should _____ the process _____.

    A   leave…alone

    B   monitor…for variation fluctuations

    C   search…for common causes

    D   investigate…for special causes

Topic E: Control charts

Explanation

Control charts provide a running record of a process. They help you decide when a process is running smoothly and when it needs attention. Specifically, control charts can help you determine whether the variation occurring in a process is caused by common or special causes. Remember that common causes of variation are inherent to the process. They are a normal part of how the process functions, and they cause collected data to vary in a random manner. Special causes, on the other hand, are not part of the process, and they cause collected data to vary in a nonrandom manner.

Control chart analysis

Control charts are used to understand the amount of variation in a process based on the past performance of the same process. If nothing changes in a process, then past performance should be a good indicator of future performance. Control charts use this logic to help you determine how much variation you should expect from a process. If something different, unusual, or unexpected happens in the process, the control chart highlights it so that you can research the cause.

In addition, control chart analysis might yield information about the consistency of the product characteristic being measured. It might reveal that the process is unstable or producing an unacceptable level of variation. In these cases, action is needed to improve the performance of the process.

Analysis of a control chart might also identify specific points at which the process is performing differently than expected. These points should be researched to understand what caused the unexpected performance. Another possible result of control chart analysis is discovering when a process is running smoothly and no changes are needed.

Do it!

E-1: Using a control chart

Multiple-choice questions

1 Select the choice that describes the purpose of a control chart.

A Helps determine whether a relationship exists between two variables.

B Helps prioritize problems and the causes of problems.

C Helps determine whether a variation is caused by common or special causes.

D Helps identify and categorize the possible causes of a problem.

2 Select the characteristics of control charts.

A They help you determine whether variation is caused by common or special causes.

B They help you decide when a process can be left alone.

C They help you identify cycles, trends, shifts, and mixtures.

D They help you display the variation of a process characteristic over time.

E They help you determine when a process needs adjustments.

Control chart components

Explanation

The main components of a control chart include a centerline, which represents the process, and data points that are collected from the process. Control charts also consist of statistically-determined upper and lower boundaries of expected process performance. The upper boundary is known as the *upper control limit*, and the lower boundary is known as the *lower control limit*. Exhibit 4-10 shows these components.

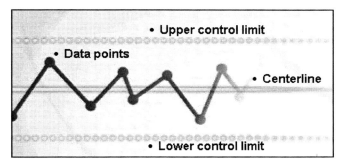

Exhibit 4-10: Components of a control chart

Importance of control charts

Using control charts is important because they can help you determine when a process can be left alone and when it might need adjustment. When a control chart reveals that something has happened that you would not expect based on past performance, such as when one or more points fall outside the chart's upper or lower control limits, the process is out of control. If that happens, you should investigate to identify the special cause that produced this condition. When a control chart reveals that the process is behaving as expected—meaning that no points fall outside the chart's upper or lower control limits—the process is in control.

A process that is in control is said to be stable. A *stable process* will continue to provide predictable results unless something changes in the process. In many cases, this level of performance is acceptable, so all that is left for you to do is continue to monitor the performance of the process on the control chart. In other cases, the level of performance might not be acceptable. For example, the process might produce the product or service in 30 to 90 minutes, but customers might be willing to wait only 45 minutes. In cases where the level of performance is not acceptable, you will need to design a new process capable of satisfying your customers' requirements.

Unit summary: Understanding current performance

Topic A
In this unit, you learned how to **create flow charts** in order to document a process. You learned about the symbols used to create flow charts, as well as some benefits of using them. You also learned that different types of flow charts, such as **functional flow charts** and **layout flow charts**, can help you understand processes in different ways.

Topic B
You also learned that **check sheets** record the frequency of various events. You learned how to create different types of check sheets, as well as how to avoid common pitfalls during data collection.

Topic C
Next, you learned how to create **histograms**, which show variance in a process. You learned that histograms with little variance have a small number of tall bars, while those with greater variance have many shorter bars. You also learned how to interpret various shapes in histograms.

Topic D
Then you learned how to create **run charts**, which display variation in a process characteristic over time. You learned to identify common run chart patterns, including **cycles**, **mixtures**, **trends**, and **shifts**.

Topic E
Finally, you learned that **control charts** provide a running record of a process, and can help show whether variation is due to common or special causes. You learned the components and importance of control charts.

Review questions

Icon's Chief Finance Officer (CFO) has directed that all invoices must be paid within 30 days, unless there are specific reasons not to do so. Paying within 30 days will enable Icon to maintain a good credit rating, receive discounts, and avoid late fees or finance charges. Recently, several invoices have been paid after the 30-day period.

In the invoice approval process, the accounts payable (AP) clerk must get approval for invoices from either the manager of the department that ordered the expenditure or the accounting manager. Any invoice over a certain amount also has to be approved by the Vice President who oversees the department or the CFO.

1 The first step to outline the invoice approval process with a flow chart is to put the word "Start" in a symbol. Which shape is generally used for this purpose?

   a A square.

   b A rectangle.

   c A circle.

   d An oval.

2 The first step in the invoice approval process occurs when the mailroom receives the invoice. How should this activity be displayed?

   a With a rectangle.

   b With a circle.

   c With a diamond.

   d With a square.

3 After the AP clerk receives the invoice, he or she needs to decide if it needs the approval of the department manager. Such decision points are represented by diamonds in a flow chart. From the following options, what would be the best question to ask at this point?

   a Where should the invoice go next?

   b Does the invoice need the department manager's approval?

   c Which department manager needs to approve it?

   d Is the invoice over the department manager's approval limit?

4 When creating a flow chart, what should you do after a decision point?

   a Draw one arrow labeled "yes" and another labeled "no".

   b Draw two dotted lines labeled "yes" and "no".

   c Decide which choice is most commonly made.

   d Decide which choice is correct.

5 The following flow chart outlines the procedure for approving an invoice and details when a specific department is responsible for the expenditures. One of the benefits of a flow chart is that it shows employees how they fit into the process. For example, if you were a department manager, what information could you tell from the flow chart shown in Exhibit 4-11?

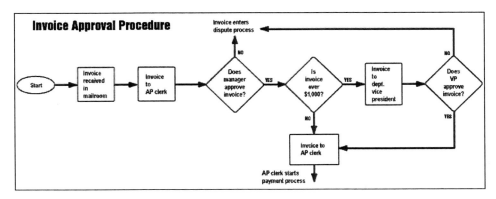

Exhibit 4-11: Sample flow chart

a That I will not review invoices that are over $1,000 because they are routed to a vice president.

b That a vice president will be involved in the process anytime I dispute an invoice.

c That I can approve invoices up to $1,000 without a vice president's approval.

d That I will make the decision as to whether I see the invoice or if it goes through the accounting approval procedure.

6 Another benefit of using a flow chart is that variance in work performance is shown. For example, suppose that the events in the following list were all occurring in work performance. Which event doesn't follow the process documented in Exhibit 4-11?

a The mailroom is routing all invoices to the AP clerk.

b A department manager is sending all approved invoices under $1,000 directly to the AP clerk.

c A vice president is sending disputed invoices to the department manager.

d A vice president is routing approved invoices over $1,000 to the AP clerk.

7 Management is concerned that the time needed for approvals is too long. One reason it might take so long is that a number of people see an invoice before it's approved. Including someone in the mailroom, what is the maximum number of people who might handle an invoice before it's approved or enters a dispute process?

a Three

b Five

c Four

d Two

8 After looking at the flow chart in Exhibit 4-11, a team decides to use a check sheet to gather data to determine if there was a problem with the approval process. The first step for creating a check sheet is to decide what data to collect. Looking at the check sheet in Exhibit 4-12, which data did the team decide to collect?

Time Needed for Invoice Approval					
TIME	**Person with Final Approval**				TOTAL
	Accounting Manager	Department Manager	CFO	Dept. Vice President	
1-5 days	ⅧⅠ III	III	I		12
6-10 days	ⅧⅠ I	ⅧⅠ ⅧⅠ	ⅧⅠ	ⅧⅠ	26
11-15 days	II	ⅧⅠ	IIII	ⅧⅠ	16
15-20 days		II	II	II	6
21-25 days		I		IIII	5
TOTAL	16	21	12	16	65

Exhibit 4-12: A sample check sheet

    a The amount of time different positions needed to approve invoices.

    b The amount of time an invoice spent with each position along the process.

    c The number of different job positions that approved invoices.

    d The number of invoices each job position approved.

9 The check sheet in Exhibit 4-12 has one piece of information missing. What is it?

    a The period of time over which the data was collected

    b The names of the people with final approval

    c A detailed description of each invoice

    d The amount of each invoice

10 It's important to avoid pitfalls when collecting data and designing a check sheet. Study the check sheet in Exhibit 4-12 and identify the error that was made on it.

    a The total for the VP column was calculated incorrectly.

    b The categories were not separated correctly.

    c The labels are incorrect.

    d The total for the 6-10 days row was calculated incorrectly.

11 The team can also look at the data by using a histogram. The team determined that it would separate the data into the number of days that it took for invoices to be approved. If there were 65 data points, what would the recommended number of classes be?

   a Eight

   b Ten

   c Six

   d Four

12 If the smallest of the 65 data points in the check sheet shown in Exhibit 4-12 is one day, and the largest is 24 days, what would the width of each class be if you have eight classes?

   a Two days

   b Three days

   c Eight days

   d Five days

13 You know that there will be eight classes that have a width of three days. Also, the smallest data point is one and the largest is 24. How should you define the classes?

   a 1-3, 3-6, 6-9, 9-12, 12-15, 15-18, 18-21, 21-24

   b 1-8, 9-16, 17-24

   c 1-3, 4-6, 7-9, 10-12, 13-15, 16-18, 19-21, 22-24

   d 0-3, 4-7, 8-11, 12-15, 16-19, 20-23, 24-27

14 After defining the classes, what is the next step in creating a histogram?

   a Determine the number of classes on the vertical axis.

   b Count the number of occurrences in each class.

   c Draw the vertical bars to represent the data.

   d Determine the width of the classes on the vertical axis.

Unit 5

Causes of problems

Unit time: 40 minutes

Complete this unit, and you'll know how to:

A Create and interpret a cause-and-effect diagram.

B Create and analyze a Pareto chart.

C Create and interpret a scatter diagram.

D Create an interrelationship diagram and use it to identify root causes.

Topic A: Cause-and-effect diagrams

Explanation

Cause-and-effect diagrams, also known as "fishbone" or "Ishikawa" diagrams, are used to identify and categorize the possible causes of a problem and to help discover its root (as shown in Exhibit 5-1). Cause-and-effect diagrams provide the most benefit when used as a tool to help teams brainstorm. *Brainstorming* is a process that helps generate many ideas in a small amount of time. It is important that the team consist of individuals who fully understand the process.

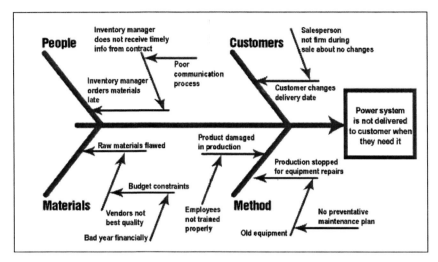

Exhibit 5-1: A sample cause-and-effect diagram

Cause-and-effect diagrams force team members to think of possible causes of a problem in multiple categories. This approach is beneficial because it can prevent team members from focusing too heavily on one particular area of a process, while failing to examine other areas. For example, a team could become so focused on finding problem causes related to materials that they forget to examine environmental factors.

Creating cause-and-effect diagrams

There are four steps you should complete to create a cause-and-effect diagram:

1   **Determine the problem you want to investigate.** On the right side of a piece of paper, record a concise statement that identifies the problem. Then, draw a box around the statement and create an arrow pointing toward the box.

2   **Identify the main causes of the stated problem.** Write these causes on diagonal arrows pointing toward the main arrow. If you have difficulty identifying main causes, use the following general categories: Environment, People, Method, Machine, Materials, and Measurement.

3 **Identify causes for the main causes.** The second-level causes can be added to the cause-and-effect diagram by writing them on arrows pointing toward the main cause arrows. This process should be repeated as long as necessary until you feel certain that all possible causes are recorded. Third- and fourth-level causes can be added by simply drawing more arrows on the diagram. Keep in mind that a cause can be repeated in various places if needed.

4 **Take action based on what is discovered.** Unless you take action to make improvements after problem causes have been identified, the cause-and-effect diagram will provide no benefits.

If a cause-and-effect diagram becomes difficult to read because there are many levels of causes, transfer each cause you want to further analyze to a separate diagram. The transferred cause should now be listed in the box at the right side of the new diagram, and additional levels of causes can be added. This approach provides more space for recording additional causes and the arrows needed to convey the relationships between the levels.

In addition to constructing multiple cause-and-effect diagrams, you can use interrelationship diagrams to examine the causes of a problem. Interrelationship diagrams are easier to read than cause-and-effect diagrams when there are numerous causes to be examined, and they provide an analysis of the relationships that exist among the causes.

Do it!

A-1: Creating a cause-and-effect diagram

Exercises

1 Select the choice that best describes why cause-and-effect diagrams help teams think of numerous causes of a problem.

    A They examine the relationships among causes.

    B They prioritize the causes of a problem.

    C They force teams to think in multiple categories.

    D They analyze the relationships between process variables.

2 Identify and sequence the steps required to create a cause-and-effect diagram.

Identify the main causes.

Circle the causes.

Determine problem to investigate.

Identify the causes for the main causes.

Analyze the relationships among the causes.

Take action.

3 Choose a problem or an effect from the following list:

- Invoice errors
- Missing the promised delivery date
- High manpower turnover
- Losing control of car
- Winning a tennis match
- Recurring failure of a hydraulic machine

Follow the steps to create an outline of the cause-and-effect diagram for the problem or effect you choose.

Variations of the cause-and-effect diagram

Explanation

There are several variations of the cause-and-effect diagram that can offer additional help in identifying problem causes. One variation is to determine an effect that you want to see happen. List this effect in the box at the right side of a cause-and-effect diagram and identify actions that could cause the effect to occur. Add these main causes to the diagram and then continue listing causes for the main causes and so forth. Using this variation can be helpful because it is frequently easier for people to work toward achieving a new goal instead of trying to decide how to fix a problem.

A second variation of the cause-and-effect diagram is to have a team brainstorm possible causes that could contribute to a problem or an effect. After a list of causes has been created, the team can start classifying the relationships among the causes by making a diagram like the standard cause-and-effect diagram. Although this option might produce a diagram similar to what might be created by using the standard method, listing all the possible causes without having to identify relationships at the same time might help some teams.

A third variation of the cause-and-effect diagram can encourage broad participation in the process. To gain input from more than just a team, a cause-and-effect diagram can be posted in a public area in the workplace, so all employees can add their ideas. This method can be accomplished by using a large white board or covering a bulletin board with blank paper. Write in the problem or effect, and leave the diagram displayed for about two weeks. Invite all employees to offer their thoughts about the causes. This approach provides an organization with extensive information about how to solve a problem or accomplish a goal. By involving all employees, a wide range of ideas will be obtained.

Issues affecting creation of cause-and-effect diagrams

There are two issues that affect a team's ability to create an effective cause-and-effect diagram.

- **Facilitation.** The cause-and-effect diagram leads to special problems because the person recording the information will need to create one- or two-word statements that will fit on an arrow to summarize each cause that is identified. In addition, the facilitator must determine where the cause should be placed. Frequently, the best approach is to allow the entire team to have input.

- **Review time.** It is important to allow team members time to review the diagram they have created. It is best for the review to happen the following day, so team members can step away and come back with a fresh perspective. Upon review, team members might think of new causes for the problem or effect, or might discover that a cause has been put in the wrong position.

Do it!

A-2: Reviewing a cause-and-effect diagram

Multiple-choice question

1 If you and a team had just completed a cause-and-effect diagram, when should the team schedule time to review it?

A Immediately

B After a short break

C The following week

D The following day

Topic B: Pareto charts

Explanation

A *Pareto chart* is a specialized bar graph that can be used to prioritize problems or problem causes (as shown in Exhibit 5-2). In other words, Pareto charts help identify which problems or causes are most important; therefore, they identify where improvement efforts should be made to provide the greatest benefit. Without this focus, individuals might be tempted to focus on problems that seem the worst or attract the most attention but are in fact not the most pressing issues.

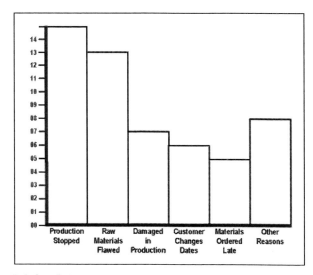

Exhibit 5-2: A sample Pareto chart

Pareto charts are based on the *Pareto Principle*, which is named for the nineteenth-century Italian economist Vilfredo Pareto. The basis of the Pareto Principle is that roughly 80 percent of effects are produced by 20 percent of the causes. In terms of quality management, this theory can be translated to 80 percent of problems are produced by 20 percent of the machines, materials, employees, or other causes. Thus, Pareto charts, as quality leader Joseph M. Juran stated, separate the "vital few" from the "trivial many."

Creating Pareto charts

There is a five-step process you should follow to create a Pareto chart:

1 **Identify the categories for which you want to collect data.** The data might be divided into categories of various problems or categories of various problem causes.

2 **Collect data.** The data you want to analyze should be collected over a specified period of time.

3 **Sort the categories according to frequency of occurrence.** For example, suppose you are collecting data about the locations of damage caused to computer monitors while being shipped. Suppose the categories include Monitor's Face, Monitor's Left Side, and Monitor's Right Side. To complete the third step of the process for this example, you would need to determine which category had the most occurrences of damage, which had the second most, and so on.

4 **Label the axes of the chart.** The categories should be listed in descending order on the horizontal axis. Use a scale appropriate for the collected data on the vertical axis.

5 **Draw the bars.**

Analyzing Pareto charts

The tallest bars in a Pareto chart indicate which categories are most important. Improvement efforts focused on these categories will provide the most benefit. You should keep in mind that the categories represented by the shorter bars are not unimportant. Quality improvement efforts should be applied to these categories as well, but only after the issues represented by taller bars have been solved.

Do it!
B-1: Creating and analyzing a Pareto chart

Exercises

1 Sequence the steps to create a Pareto chart.

Collect data over specified time period.

Draw the bars.

Identify the categories.

Sort the categories.

Label the axes of the chart.

2 Select the category on the Pareto chart that would provide the most benefit when improvement efforts are applied to it.

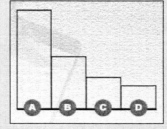

A   Category A

B   Category B

C   Category C

D   Category D

3   Avenue Electronics, a TV manufacturing company, wants to reduce the incidences of customer complaints recorded within the warranty period. The data gathered for the parts replaced over a three-month period is as follows.

DATA SHEET

Avenue Electronics: Component replacement within warranty period
Data gathered by: Jim Cassella
Model: 528C
Period: 1st March 2002 to 31st May 2002

Parts replaced	March 2002	April 2002	May 2002	Total
Switches	6	7	8	21
Capacitors	12	15	17	44
Transformers	1	2	1	4
CRT	1		1	2
Integrated circuit	3	4	5	12
Resistors	2	3	1	6
Other parts	3	7	5	15
Total	28	38	38	104

Prepare a Pareto chart and then identify the category on which you should focus improvement efforts (to reduce the number of complaints).

4   Discuss how Avenue Electronics should proceed to reduce the warranty cost.

Topic C: Scatter diagram

Explanation

A *scatter diagram* is used to determine whether a relationship exists between two variables of a process. For example, you might want to see if there is a relationship between the number of overtime hours worked and the number of mistakes made. The scatter chart shown in Exhibit 5-3 attempts to show a relationship between the number of new employees and the number of customer complaints received.

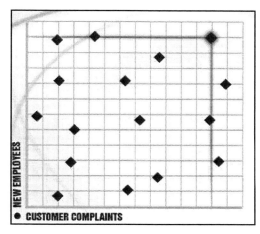

Exhibit 5-3: A sample scatter diagram

Creating scatter diagrams

You can create a scatter diagram by following a three-step process:

1 **Collect data about both variables.** Each variable must be measured over the same time period.

2 **Label the axes.** You should label the horizontal axis with a scale appropriate for one variable, the vertical axis with a scale appropriate for the other.

3 **Plot the points.** Each point represents the place where the two variables intersect. At each intersection, draw a small dot or other symbol. For the customer complaint example shown in Exhibit 5-3, one axis shows the number of new employees, and the other axis shows the number of complaints received. Suppose that the week you received 24 customer complaints you had 11 new employees working. You would find the point on the graph representing 24 complaints and 11 new employees and draw a small dot there.

Interpreting scatter diagrams

When your scatter diagram is complete, you need to analyze the relationship between the two variables. To do so, you must understand the kinds of data relationships depicted on the diagram. Possible data relationships include the following:

- **No correlation.** Randomly scattered data points indicate that the variables are unrelated, as shown in Exhibit 5-4.

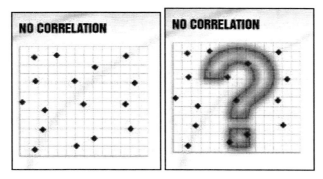

Exhibit 5-4: Sample scatter diagrams showing no correlation

- **Positive correlation.** Data points in an upward-sloping line indicate that when one variable increases, the other variable also increases, as shown in Exhibit 5-5.

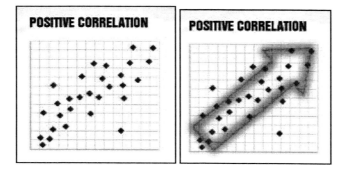

Exhibit 5-5: Sample scatter diagrams showing positive correlation

- **Negative correlation.** Data points in a downward-sloping line indicate that when one variable increases, the other variable decreases, as shown in Exhibit 5-6.

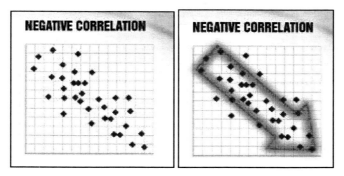

Exhibit 5-6: Sample scatter diagrams showing negative correlation

- **Curvilinear correlation.** Data points in a U-shaped curve indicate that the relationship between the variables fluctuates between positive and negative correlation, as shown in Exhibit 5-7.

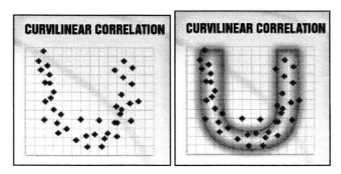

Exhibit 5-7: Sample scatter diagrams showing curvilinear correlation

Strength of correlation

The strength of the correlation between the variables is indicated by the compactness of the plotted points. The more tightly packed the points are to a line, the stronger the correlation. The more scattered the points are, the weaker the correlation. Exhibit 5-8 shows examples of weak and strong correlation.

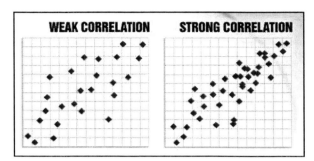

Exhibit 5-8: Sample scatter diagrams showing weak and strong correlation

Scatter diagram pitfalls

There are several pitfalls related to the interpretation of scatter diagrams. When a correlation between the two variables is indicated, it is important to know that this is not proof that one of the variables caused the results in the other variable. There might be a relationship between the variables, but it is not necessarily cause-and-effect. In addition, even when two variables on a scatter diagram do not appear to be related, they might still be. For example, a measurement error could prevent you from seeing the correlation.

To ensure that your scatter diagrams are accurate and to avoid these pitfalls, you should be sure you have at least 20 to 25 data points so that your sample is large enough to be statistically valid. You should also involve people who understand the process from which the variables are taken. These people can include operators, engineers, supervisors, and maintenance personnel. Such people can be very helpful with interpretation of the data. For example, if a scatter diagram indicates that there is a correlation between two variables, people who understand the process might understand the nature of the correlation.

Do it!

C-1:   Creating and interpreting a scatter diagram

Exercises

1   Select the scatter diagram in which the relationship between the variables is the strongest.

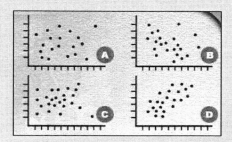

A   Scatter Diagram A

B   Scatter Diagram B

C   Scatter Diagram C

D   Scatter Diagram D

2   Match the following list of scatter diagram types with its description given below: curvilinear correlation; no correlation; absolute correlation; negative correlation; positive correlation.

The data points form a U-shaped curve.

The data points are randomly scattered.

The data points are in a downward-sloping line.

The data points are in an upward-sloping line.

Topic D: Interrelationship diagrams

Explanation

Interrelationship diagrams, also known as *interrelationship diagraphs*, are used to analyze the events that lead to a problem. Interrelationship diagrams can help you analyze the root causes of a problem because the diagrams show a graphic representation of the cause-and-effect relationships that exist among a chain of events (as shown in Exhibit 5-9).

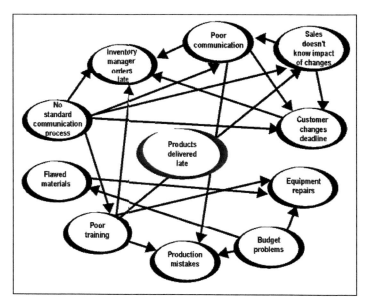

Exhibit 5-9: An interrelationship diagram

Interrelationship diagrams are similar to cause-and-effect diagrams because they examine causes of a problem. However, while cause-and-effect diagrams focus on examining different categories of causes, interrelationship diagrams analyze the relationships that exist among the causes.

Creating interrelationship diagrams

You can create an interrelationship diagram by following a five-step process:

1 **Identify a problem that needs to be analyzed.** Write the problem in the middle of the page and circle it with a bold line, so you can easily distinguish it.

2 **Make a separate list of all the causes that influence the central problem.** When your list is complete, write each cause around the first, and circle each.

3 **Analyze the relationships among the causes.** Draw an arrow from each cause to each of the effects it creates. The arrow should point toward whichever issue is the effect. Keep in mind that each cause might have multiple effects.

4 **Identify causes for the causes you have already listed.** Add the new causes to the diagram and circle them. Then, draw arrows to connect the new causes to any effects they create. Repeat this step until you can identify no more causes. At this point, your diagram can become disorganized and hard to read because there will be so many arrows pointing to circles. If your diagram becomes disorganized, do not be concerned. As long as you can determine the cause and effect relationships, your diagram will serve its purpose.

5 **Identify root causes.** Root causes have the fewest arrows pointing at them. Identifying root causes is important because they have the most influence on the problem as a whole. Therefore, changes made to the root causes will create the most pronounced improvement.

Do it!

D-1: Creating an interrelationship diagram

Exercises

1 Select the choice that is most likely to be a root cause.

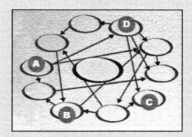

A Cause A

B Cause B

C Cause C

D Cause D

2 Identify and sequence the steps of the process for creating an interrelationship diagram.

Identify the root cause or causes.

Identify the critical path.

Identify causes for causes.

Categorize the causes.

Analyze the relationships.

Make a list of causes.

Identify the problem.

3 Discuss why it is that root causes have the fewest arrows pointing at them.

Unit summary: Causes of problems

Topic A   In this unit, you learned that **cause-and-effect** diagrams help identify and categorize causes of a problem. You learned how to create cause-and-effect diagrams, and that variations of them can be used for deriving a desired effect or for brainstorming.

Topic B   Next, you learned how to create and analyze **Pareto charts**, and that they help identify where to focus improvement efforts by prioritizing problems or problem causes.

Topic C   Then, you learned how to create **scatter diagrams**, which can show the relationship between two variables. You learned the meanings of different patterns, as well as how to determine the strength of correlation between variables.

Topic D   Finally, you learned how to create an **interrelationship** diagram, which helps determine root causes by analyzing the events that lead to a problem.

Review questions

Icon manufactures power systems that power rack-mounted computer and telecommunications equipment. The power systems are delivered to original equipment manufacturers (OEMs) that integrate Icon's systems with their own products. Lately, Icon has missed customer delivery dates. You will use diagrams and charts to identify what is causing the problem.

1 One way to look at problems is to use a cause-and-effect diagram. The first step of the process for creating such a diagram is to determine the problem you want to investigate. What other actions should be performed in this step of the process?

   a Determine which causes are most important so that the focus can be narrowed.

   b Write a short description of the problem and draw a box around it.

   c Draw arrows that will represent the main causes of the problem.

   d Determine which main causes are relevant to the problem that is being studied.

2 The second step is to identify the main causes of the problem. You can create your own categories if you wish. However, there are several categories that are commonly used. Which of the following are examples of those categories?

   a Production, Sales, Administration, and Finance

   b People, Method, Machine, and Measurement

   c Training, Hiring, Management, and Facilities

   d Product, Place, Processes, and Communication

3 After determining the main causes, the next step is to identify causes for the main causes. For instance, you discover that one of the causes of the delivery problems is that production has to be stopped frequently for equipment repairs. To which category of main cause does that problem contribute?

   a Customers

   b Materials

   c Machine

   d People

4 During a discussion of possible causes of frequent stops in production, a team member says, "We have to repair the equipment so often because the equipment is old." How should this idea be recorded on the cause-and-effect diagram?

   a As an arrow pointing to the "Production stopped…" arrow

   b On a separate sheet until the cause can be verified

   c As an arrow pointing to the "Method" arrow

   d By adding the words "because of old equipment" to the end of the "Production stopped…" arrow

5 Another way to look at problems is to use a Pareto chart. Suppose during one month, managers were asked to keep track of the number of times events occurred in several categories of problems that delayed production or delivery. After data has been collected, what should be done with the data?

   a Sort the categories according to the time they occurred.

   b Sort the categories according to the frequency of occurrence.

   c Sort the categories according to the amount of delay they caused.

   d Sort the categories according to the place they occurred.

6 After the categories are prioritized, you can label the axes of the Pareto chart. Where and how should the categories be listed?

   a In ascending order on the vertical axis

   b In ascending order on the horizontal axis

   c In descending order on the horizontal axis

   d In descending order on the vertical axis

7 Based on the analysis of the Pareto chart shown in Exhibit 5-10, to what areas should the team first apply quality improvement efforts?

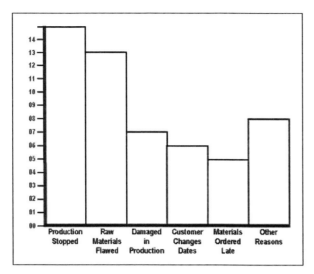

Exhibit 5-10: A sample Pareto chart

    a Customers changing dates and inventory managers ordering late

    b Flawed raw materials and damage to product in production

    c Stoppage in production and damage to product in production

    d Stoppage in production and flawed raw materials

8 The first step for creating an interrelationship diagram is to identify the problem that needs to be addressed. What is the next step?

    a Make a list of causes for the problem on the right side of the page.

    b Identify other problems that might have similar causes.

    c Develop a list of causes, determine root causes, and put them all in circles around the problem.

    d Make a list of causes for the problem and put them in circles around the problem.

9 After listing the causes of the problems, what should be your next step?

    a Draw arrows from the problem to the causes.

    b List other problems created by the causes.

    c List causes for the causes listed.

    d Draw arrows from each cause to the effect(s) it creates.

10 In an interrelationship diagram, what should you do after analyzing the relationships among causes?

   a Identify causes for the causes listed and draw arrows to the effects they create.

   b Identify the root causes by looking for the circles that have the most arrows pointing to them.

   c Identify the root causes by looking for circles that have the most arrows pointing away from them.

   d Identify causes for the causes and list them on another paper as your root causes.

11 The final step for creating an interrelationship diagram is to identify root causes. In the interrelationship diagram shown in Exhibit 5-11, what two causes should be identified as root causes?

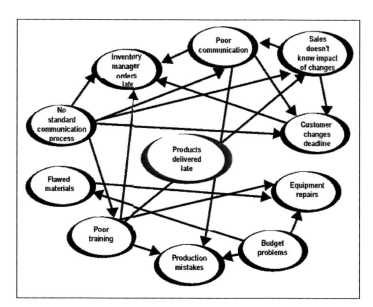

Exhibit 5-11: A sample interrelationship diagram

   a Poor training and poor communication

   b No standard communication process and budget problems

   c Budget problems and poor communication

   d Flawed materials and poor communication

Unit 6

Ideas and organization

Unit time: 50 minutes

Complete this unit, and you'll know how to:

A Sequence and follow the steps for brainstorming.

B Identify the purpose of affinity diagrams.

C Construct activity network diagrams.

D Identify the benefits of using CPM and PERT charts to understand the critical path of a project.

Topic A: Brainstorming

Explanation

Brainstorming works best when used by a group of four to nine people. When brainstorming, team members' goals should be to break their existing patterns of thought by generating original and creative ideas.

Process of brainstorming

The process for brainstorming includes five steps:

1 **Choose the purpose of the brainstorming session.** There are two purposes a team can have for brainstorming: generating either a list of causes of or solutions to a problem. Typically, a team would schedule one brainstorming session to identify causes for a problem, and then schedule another to identify solutions.

2 **Organize for the brainstorming session.** The team should determine how they will record ideas and who will record them. During brainstorming, the ideas generated by the team should be visible to the entire group because examining the list can help team members generate more ideas. For this reason, a flip chart is often the best way to record ideas. The flip chart can be placed within everyone's view, and when a page is full, it can be hung on the wall.

3 **Review the rules for the session.** Successful brainstorming requires adherence to three basic rules:

   - Neither verbal nor nonverbal criticism should be allowed.

   - Ideas should not be evaluated during the brainstorming session.

   - Imaginative ideas should be encouraged.

   Following these rules is essential because the goal of a brainstorming session is to compile a list of as many ideas as possible. If team members feel their ideas might be subject to criticism and immediate evaluation, they are likely to withhold them. In addition, outrageous ideas can be valuable in brainstorming because they can lead other team members to create additional ideas. Therefore, team members should be encouraged to share all ideas even if they seem unusual or impractical.

4 **Begin generating ideas.** Everyone must be allowed to participate equally in this step. To ensure equal participation, the team can suggest ideas one-by-one, taking turns until everyone is out of ideas.

5 **Ask questions and clarify ideas.** This step should be completed when the team has finished generating ideas. Use clarification and questions only to ensure that everyone understands each of the ideas suggested. This step does not include evaluating the ideas, and team members shouldn't argue for or against specific ideas while brainstorming. Keep in mind that brainstorming is a process that helps generate ideas that are to be evaluated at a separate time.

Do it!   **A-1:   Steps for brainstorming**

Exercises

1 Sequence the steps for brainstorming.

Begin generating ideas.

Select the purpose.

Organize for the session.

Ask questions and clarify ideas.

Review the rules.

2 Discuss which of the following topics are appropriate for a brainstorming session.

A   The population of Switzerland is 72,83,274

B   How to progress in life

C   Crack in a switch cover at the edge after drilling in machine 683

D   The increasing profitability of the company Avenue Electronics

E   The frequent breakdown of the machine 64B due to oil seal leakage

Topic B: Affinity diagrams

Explanation *Affinity diagrams* are used to help a team of five to 15 members create a large number of ideas for solving a problem, as well as to organize those ideas into categories to make them easier to manage. Creating affinity diagrams also helps a team fully understand the problem they are working to solve. In addition, the process of categorizing ideas for solutions can help the team discover new approaches for solving the problem.

Creating affinity diagrams

You should complete a four-step process to create an affinity diagram:

1 **Determine a problem or issue that needs to be resolved.** After the problem has been determined, create a statement that accurately describes the issue at hand. It is important for team members to agree on the wording of the statement to ensure that everyone views the problem in the same way. For example, your problem statement could be "It takes too long to process our employees' expense reports."

2 **Generate ideas about issues affecting the problem statement.** A team can use the normal process of brainstorming in this step. They should generate at least 20 ideas, but typical affinity diagrams are created from as many as 50 ideas, and some might have 100 or more issues. The number of ideas raised by the team will depend on the problem or issue at hand. Each idea should be recorded on a note card or sticky note. Note cards can be spread out on a table. Sticky notes can be spread out on a table or an empty wall.

3 **Sort the cards or sticky notes.** Without any discussion, the team should sort the ideas into five to 10 categories. Each team member should start moving the cards or notes as he or she thinks appropriate.

If one idea in particular continues to be moved between categories, team members should try to understand why each member is categorizing it differently. If necessary, the team can stop to clarify the meaning of that idea. If it still seems to fit into more than one category, a duplicate card or note should be made. Eventually, the sorting will slow down as members become more comfortable with the categories that have been created. Keep in mind that there might be a few ideas that do not fit in any of the categories.

4 **Determine headings for the categories.** This step is important because the headings help clarify why individuals separated the ideas in certain ways. One individual might have interpreted a particular category differently than another team member. Therefore, consensus should be reached before finalizing any category headings.

Benefits of affinity diagrams

Using affinity diagrams provides two important benefits to a team:

* Affinity diagrams encourage participation from all team members. The process of categorizing ideas in silence allows all team members to add their ideas without feeling they'll have to defend them. Banning discussion also prevents old arguments, emotions, or personal biases from inhibiting progress. In addition, all team members feel ownership in the process, and will be interested in seeing valuable results produced by it.

* Affinity diagrams facilitate problem solving by giving a team a place to start after the brainstorming process. Organizing the ideas generated in brainstorming will make possible solutions easier to discuss and analyze. Placing ideas into categories can also help a team to escape typical patterns and try new approaches.

Do it!

B-1: Using an affinity diagram

Multiple-choice question

1 Select the benefits of using affinity diagrams.

  A They enable team members to defend their ideas.

  B They facilitate problem solving.

  C They help individuals identify and overcome their personal biases.

  D They help teams resolve old arguments.

  E They encourage participation from all team members.

Topic C: Activity network diagrams

Explanation

Activity network diagrams are helpful for planning implementation of quality improvements because they divide projects into a series of activities. Activity network diagrams are also used to define the dependencies among the activities and estimate the duration for each activity.

Constructing activity network diagrams

On activity network diagrams, nodes and arrows illustrate the sequence and relationships of the activities that make up a project, as shown in Exhibit 6-1. A network starts with an activity that does not have any *predecessors* and ends with an activity that does not have any *successors*. Activity network diagrams are generally constructed so that workflow starts on the left and proceeds to the right.

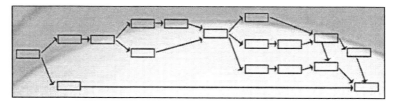

Exhibit 6-1: A sample activity network diagram

Arrow-charting methods

There are two methods of arrow charting used to create activity network diagrams:

- *Activity-on-node method*: Boxes, called *nodes*, represent activities, while arrows drawn between the nodes represent activity relationships, as shown in Exhibit 6-2.

- *Activity-on-arrow method*: Arrows represent activities, while the nodes represent events and demonstrate how activities relate to one another, as shown in Exhibit 6-3.

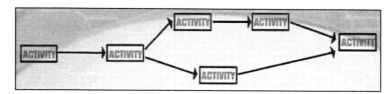

Exhibit 6-2: A sample activity-on-node diagram

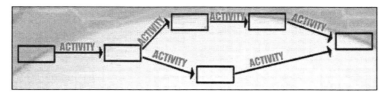

Exhibit 6-3: A sample activity-on-arrow diagram

Do it!

C-1:   Creating an activity network diagram

Multiple-choice question

1 Select the types of arrow charting that you can use to create an activity network diagram.

A   Activity-on-diagram

B   Activity-on-event

C   Activity-on-node

D   Activity-on-arrow

E   Activity-on-milestone

Topic D: CPM and PERT

Explanation

The *Critical Path Method (CPM)* and the *Program Evaluation and Review Technique (PERT)* are both techniques for network planning. Each shows a project as a sequence of activities, helping teams analyze entire projects or individual activities. Exhibit 6-4 shows samples of CPM and PERT charts.

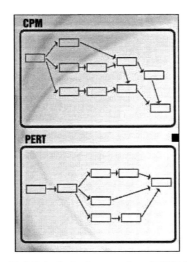

Exhibit 6-4: A sample of CPM and PERT

In addition, CPM and PERT charts can be used to analyze the relationships and dependencies among activities. In the strictest sense, CPM is charted using activity-on-node diagrams, and PERT is charted using activity-on-arrow diagrams. However, people frequently use a combination of features from both CPM and PERT.

Using CPM or PERT

Using CPM, PERT, or a combination of the two provides several benefits. For example, both systems allow you to determine whether a project can be completed by a designated time. Another benefit is that CPM and PERT can show when individual activities need to be completed to achieve the overall project deadline. In addition, both systems can show which activities have leeway for when they need to start or end, and both systems can help you determine the critical path for a project.

Critical path and critical activities

The *critical path* on a CPM or PERT chart is the longest chain of activities that cannot be completed concurrently, as shown in Exhibit 6-5. This path determines the minimum duration of the entire project.

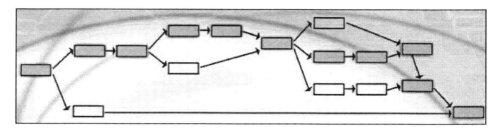

Exhibit 6-5: The critical path indicated by the gray boxes

The activities on the critical path are called critical activities because missing a deadline on even one affects all subsequent activities and the overall project deadline. Identifying the critical path and critical activities on a project schedule can help you determine how priority changes affect a project and which activities are most affected by the changes. In addition, identifying the critical path and critical activities can help you determine where you can adjust the schedule to make up for lost time.

Do it!

D-1:   Network planning

Multiple-choice question

1   Select the information you can gain by knowing the critical path of a project.

   A   It helps determine the activity that takes the most time.

   B   It helps determine how priority changes affect a project.

   C   It helps determine whether to use CPM or PERT.

   D   It helps determine which activities are most affected by changes.

   E   It helps determine where you can adjust the schedule.

Unit summary: Ideas and organization

Topic A   In this unit, you learned how to use the process of **brainstorming** to generate many ideas quickly.

Topic B   Next, you learned how teams can use **affinity diagrams** to generate and categorize ideas for solving problems. You learned that affinity diagrams encourage participation from all team members and facilitate problem solving.

Topic C   Then, you learned how to use **activity network** diagrams to plan quality improvements by dividing a project into a series of activities. You also learned about the types of arrow charting used to create activity network diagrams.

Topic D   Finally, you learned about two techniques of **network planning**, **CPM** and **PERT**. You also learned to use CPM and PERT charts to identify the **critical path** and **critical activities**.

Review questions

You have been requested to join a brainstorming session to determine the reasons for a high rate of defects in the insulated wiring, which Icon manufactures and sells, to original equipment manufacturers (OEMs). The other people attending the session are Cindy Becker, Customer Support Specialist; Ronald Spear, Plant Supervisor; and Dean Kramer, Production Manager. As the Quality Assurance Director, you are expected to generate ideas on the causes of the defects.

Objectives:

- Follow the steps for brainstorming.
- Identify the purpose of affinity diagrams.

You kick off the session by going over the ground rules of a brainstorming session. First, a person should be designated to record all the ideas generated. Second, a brainstorming session is about thinking of as many causes as possible. There should be no evaluation or criticism of any idea. Third, all members must participate equally.

Ronald agrees to record the proceedings of the session. You request Cindy to start the session by sharing an idea. Cindy suggests that the raw material Icon uses might be defective. Ronald agrees and adds that the machinery used for production could be defective, too. Dean remarks that the manufacturing process itself might need some optimization as some product changes had been made two months ago. You steer the direction of ideas by raising the issue of improper training for employees to handle the new product changes. Cindy agrees and asks you if the Human Resources Department would hold skill development sessions for employees. You bring the session back on track by reminding her that the purpose of the session is to generate a list of possible causes, not solutions.

Ronald makes a comment on Cindy's ideas. You remind Roland that the session is not meant to criticize and ask him to focus on the task at hand. Cindy says that she is done with generating ideas. You sense that Cindy might feel intimidated and encourage her to share all ideas. Cindy relaxes and adds that employees doing overtime might be a cause of poor quality. By now, Ronald and Dean feel that they are done with the session. You wind up by asking Cindy, Ronald, and Dean if they understand each of the ideas generated. Ronald and Cindy clear their understanding of the ideas with Dean.

Ronald asks you if you will use an affinity diagram to organize the ideas. You reply that an affinity diagram is used to organize a larger number of ideas. Dean expresses that he is unaware of the concept of an affinity diagram. Cindy explains that all team members sit down with all the ideas and organize them into categories. Team members do this in silence to avoid conflict on the categorization of ideas. Dean understands the concept and asks you if he can start creating an affinity diagram. You remind him that the team must take a break from the ideas generated and come back to analyze them later. This helps the mind to better assimilate the ideas and organize them properly.

You schedule a meeting for the following morning. Cindy, Ronald, and Dean leave with the intention of letting their minds absorb all the ideas generated in the session.

1 During a brainstorming session, you observe that ideas of some team members are absurd and irrelevant. The session facilitator asks the team member to keep silent. Is the session facilitator right?

   a Yes

   b No

2 Half an hour into a brainstorming session, you observe that 18 ideas have been collected. You feel that there is enough time left in the session, scheduled for an hour, to make an analysis and arrive at conclusions. Should you proceed to organize the ideas?

   a Yes

   b No

3 You are facilitating a brainstorming session comprising eight members. You should:

   a Let the session take its own way, and allow people to say whatever they want.

   b Let each member speak one idea at a time, taking turns.

   c Assert that everyone should behave professionally, let others speak, and not evaluate or criticize others' points.

   d Make a point and invite each member's comments on it.

4 Select the purpose of affinity diagrams.

    a They document the steps of a process.

    b They help teams create and organize ideas for solving a problem.

    c They record the frequency of occurrence of various events.

    d They divide projects into a series of activities.

5 While creating an affinity diagram:

    a The session facilitator is given the freedom to organize the ideas.

    b All team members can discuss the organization of ideas.

    c Team members organize one idea at a time, turn by turn.

    d Each team member works alone, in silence, to organize the ideas.

Unit 7

Preparing to change processes

Unit time: 45 minutes

Complete this unit, and you'll know how to:

A Identify management goals in preparation to lead business process improvement, as well as plan improvements.

Topic A: Management's role

Explanation

Business process improvement is a basic managerial responsibility. Just as managers are responsible for employee performance appraisals and budgeting, they are also responsible for making continual improvements in their division or department.

Because improving business processes is an ongoing effort, management needs to control and coordinate processes to ensure their success. In addition, employees who are affected by improvement changes need active support from management.

Management's responsibilities

There are many responsibilities management needs to fulfill:

- Management needs to determine which processes should be improved and organize personnel to implement the improvements.
- As new improvement initiatives begin, management must communicate their importance to employees. To do so, management should distribute documents that explain business process improvement.
- As changes are implemented, management should regularly update employees about the progress.
- Managers must resolve conflicts that arise, as well as recognize employees whose efforts supported the implementation process.
- After improvements are implemented, management should evaluate the process and determine what difference the improvements have made.

Do it!

A-1: Understanding management's responsibilities

Multiple-choice question

1 As business process improvements are being implemented in a company, what are some of the responsibilities of management?

   A Direct teams toward the correct solution.

   B Update employees regularly about progress.

   C Recognize employees' efforts.

   D Resolve conflicts.

   E Evaluate the improvement process.

Business process improvement

Explanation

Management needs to achieve three goals to prepare for leading business process improvement:

- Learn about business process improvement.
- Assess new improvement initiatives.
- Champion business process improvement.

Learn about business process improvement

Managers must educate themselves about business process improvement and the techniques that can be used to implement changes. This will help strengthen management's commitment to continual improvement. Commitment and knowledge are essential as managers coach employees through changes.

Assess new improvement initiatives

Management must assess cross-functional improvement initiatives. If improvements need to be made to a process that involves several departments, the managers of each department need to share their views on the project. They should discuss the strengths and weaknesses of improvement efforts, determine what problems are likely to occur, and identify what factors will contribute to the project's success.

The managers are likely to have varying concerns about implementing changes to the current process. If so, they should discuss these differences of opinion to form a clear picture of everyone's expectations for the process improvements. The managers need to come to an agreement about what they expect from the process, which will allow them to anticipate potential problems and present a united plan to the rest of the organization.

Champion business process improvement

Managers must become champions for business process improvement. The members of management need to be fully committed to making improvement an ongoing process in their departments. Managers need to encourage their employees to adopt an attitude that accepts change as a normal part of business. Because employees will look to management to demonstrate a commitment to process improvement, this commitment requires action, not just words.

Do it!

A-2:   Preparing for leading process improvement

Multiple-choice question

1 Which of the following goals should management accomplish to prepare for leading business process improvement?

A   Ensure that everyone agrees with process improvement.

B   Learn about business process improvement.

C   Champion business process improvement.

D   Select process improvement team members.

E   Assess new improvement initiatives.

Planning for improvements

Planning for the implementation of improvements is one of management's most important responsibilities. Because planning can determine the success or failure of an improvement, managers should plan for every contingency.

Managers need to plan and organize the steps required to achieve the desired improvements. Planning helps management define the goals they want to accomplish and how they can accomplish them. It also helps them sequence the steps necessary to implement changes, as well as to determine and procure the resources that will be needed.

There are four steps management should complete to plan for improvements:

1 **Identify potential processes.** The managers should make a list of all the essential business processes in the organization, or the processes that enable the business to function. When the list is complete, management should consider whether any of the processes listed are actually subprocesses of another process, as well as whether any processes are missing. One way to ensure the list is complete is to think of individual activities that consume a lot of resources. Check to see that the processes listed encompass those activities.

2 **Select processes for improvement.** Selecting a process is critical to the successful implementation of improvements. The potential outcome of these improvements must motivate employees and managers to persevere through the implementation process.

3 **Establish objectives.** This will help management come to a decision about what improvements they want to accomplish. Objectives ensure that managers have the same expectations for the improvement efforts, and can be used to give direction to the employees responsible for carrying out the implementation.

   For example, management might establish an objective to reduce the time required to produce a certain report from six hours to two hours, or to reduce the number of customer complaints by 20 percent. Management should expect their objectives to change as more information is gathered about implementing changes.

4 **Communicate to employees.** Every employee should understand how the upcoming changes will affect him or her. Management should start by issuing an announcement to all employees that states the goals of the improvement effort. To help employees adjust to expected changes, management should consider creating and distributing a document that answers employee questions and concerns. This can help to put employees at ease by reducing initial confusion and uncertainty. Communication through the normal organizational channels—meetings, newsletters, and training sessions, for example—should continue throughout the process as well.

Do it!

A-3: Planning for improvements

Exercise

1 Identify and sequence the steps management should complete to plan for improvements.

   Select team members.

   Ask department heads for team members.

   Select processes for improvement.

   Communicate to employees.

   Identify potential processes.

   Establish objectives.

Criteria for selecting a process

Explanation
There are five criteria management should consider when determining which process to improve:

- Customer satisfaction
- Condition
- Convenience
- Cost
- Compensation

Customer satisfaction

Management should consider how the current process affects internal and external customer satisfaction. They must determine whether improving the process will make a difference to customers, as well as whether a change would be strategically important. If external customers are experiencing problems, issuing complaints, returning goods, or making warranty claims, and if internal customers are having problems as well, the process is a good candidate for improvement.

Condition

Management should also consider the current condition of the process. They should determine how much is wrong with the process and whether improvement efforts could address the deficiencies of the process. Tasks that have to be repeated regularly, those that take longer to complete than necessary, or important tasks that are overlooked all point to possible areas for improvement.

Convenience

Management should discover whether developments in technology exist that could conveniently improve the process. In addition, they should perform benchmarking to help determine whether better processes exist in the industry for completing the same work. For example, you might read in a trade magazine about the efficient shipping process performed by one of the companies in your industry. You could then choose to benchmark their process to discover ways to improve your own.

A company should consider convenience early in its efforts to improve quality, when it is common to find problems that are relatively easy to solve. These quick fixes can help give improvement efforts credibility and gain employee confidence. Such solutions are sometimes called "low hanging fruit" because they are somewhat obvious and easy to achieve.

Cost

Management should determine whether costs can be dramatically reduced by altering the process or shortening its cycle. If so, the process is a good candidate for improvements. In addition to considering the cost of the existing process, management should consider the cost the company will incur if the improvement efforts are not successful.

Compensation

Management should determine whether improvements made to the process have the potential to improve competitiveness, increase market share, reduce costs, and provide opportunities for employee growth. If improvements efforts will provide valuable compensation for the organization, the process is a good candidate for improvement.

Do it!

A-4: Selecting a process

Multiple-choice questions

1 Which benefits can a company gain by completing convenient fixes early in its improvement efforts?

  A Visibility

  B Credibility

  C More personnel

  D Employee confidence

  E More funding

2 Select the criteria management should consider when determining which process to improve.

  A Cost

  B Customer satisfaction

  C Compensation

  D Configuration

  E Complexity

  F Condition

  G Convenience

Unit summary: Preparing to change processes

Topic A

In this unit, you learned about the **management's responsibilities** in business process improvement. You also learned how to plan for improvements, and the criteria managers should consider when selecting a process for improvement.

Review questions

You are the Quality Assurance Director for Icon and are responsible for developing, implementing, and coordinating product assurance programs. The intention of these programs is to prevent or eliminate defects in new and existing products. You meet Caroline Harris, Creative Director, and Linda Autry, Assistant Division Manager, to discuss the quality improvement initiatives in the company.

Objectives:

- Prepare management to lead the business process improvement.
- Identify the steps of the process for planning improvement.

As soon as the meeting begins, Linda, the Assistant Division Manager, voices her concerns about the timing of the quality initiative. Her concern is valid: quality is always important, but what is the reason for this sudden initiative to involve managers?

Caroline seems to know the answer to that. She feels that managers need to take the lead and expand the horizons for the company. In addition, they need to encourage employees to take the lead in quality consciousness as well.

You highlight the need for management to act as both leaders and catalysts in the quality initiative. Implementation of any organization-level initiative includes making the employees aware of the initiative, the impact of the initiative on their roles, its benefits, and their responsibilities.

Linda and Caroline begin to see your point. They agree that each department must make its staff aware of the initiative and their roles in it. However, the interdependency of the various departments means that a global effort for heightening awareness needs to be implemented. Now, Linda and Caroline start seeing what you intended them to see, and they suggest that a single cross-functional initiative would work best.

You re-emphasize that employees will commit to an initiative only when the management commits to it. Employees tend to tune in to their managers' attitudes, adopting a positive or negative stance accordingly. Therefore, it is extremely important for managers to adopt a positive attitude toward business process improvement.

Linda puts it succinctly: process improvement is all about recognizing, understanding, and overseeing a system of interconnected processes for a particular objective. However, Linda still has some concerns. She says that the task is easier said than done. The process of implementing change isn't easy.

You respond by highlighting the steps involved in implementing process improvement: identify potential processes for improvement, set objectives for lower level managers and employees to meet, communicate the objectives and what is required from people. The bottom line: a committed management catalyses process improvement by example and by setting clear objectives for subordinates to meet.

1 Quality initiatives are more relevant these days than ever before because:

   a Companies are producing more defective products and services than before.

   b Increased competition has made the margin for errors smaller than before.

   c Customers are more quality conscious than before.

   d Suppliers tend to supply more defective raw materials than before.

2 Management needs to be involved in quality improvement initiatives because (select all that apply):

   a Employees respond to a change in process only after observing the commitment of the management to that change.

   b Management leads the way in adopting change, and implementing new initiatives.

   c Quality improvement is essentially a management concept.

   d Management has the capability to communicate process improvement initiatives and assign responsibilities to employees.

3 Which of the following statements is correct?

   a Each department must work alone to implement quality improvement initiatives.

   b Each department must request meetings and interviews with all other departments and collate the results for itself.

   c Related departments must collaborate and share data on a quality improvement initiative and apply the results as required by customers (internal and external).

   d The management must ask departments to collect data and then advise on the best path to take.

4 The steps involved in implementing process improvement include (select all that apply):

   a Identifying potential processes for improvement.

   b Designating a specific employee to identify the limitations of the existing process.

   c Communicating the objectives of the improvement initiative to employees.

   d Convening a meeting of the Board of Directors to appraise them of the initiative.

   e Cross functional initiatives due to the interdependency of various departments.

Unit 8

A path for change

Unit time: 40 minutes

Complete this unit, and you'll know how to:

A Identify the qualifications and responsibilities of a process manager, as well as the steps for establishing a process improvement team.

B Use flow charts in business process improvement.

Topic A: Process managers

Explanation

Management should appoint a process manager for each process that will be improved. Process managers, also known as process leaders or process owners, identify ways to improve a process to meet management's goals, and then carry out the improvements.

For example, suppose management identifies a need for customer complaints to be addressed more quickly. The process manager's job would be to analyze the current process, identify areas for improvement within the process, and carry out those improvements.

Process managers are essential because no one person in an organization is responsible for an entire process. Most employees are involved with only a portion of the entire process, so they feel the other parts are beyond their control and responsibility.

Qualifications

Typically, the role of the process manager is assumed by the lower-level manager whose department is responsible for performing the largest portion of the process to be improved. This manager usually possesses three critical qualifications for the role:

- Investment in the success of improvement efforts
- Knowledge of the process
- The skills needed to lead improvement efforts

A process manager needs to have an investment in ensuring the success of improvement efforts. This will ensure that he or she considers the improvements to be important. The person who most wants to see a process improve is someone who has encountered problems with the process or who will benefit if the process is improved. Both of these criteria apply to the manager whose department works with the process every day.

The process manager must have knowledge of the process, because it would be difficult for someone to improve something that he or she does not understand. The manager who is familiar with the process from start to finish will be able to identify areas in need of improvement. He or she might also be able to anticipate how changes will affect the process.

The process manager must also have the authority to effect changes on the process and to lead others in improvement efforts. Because a process might spread through many levels and departments, the process manager needs the position, status, and good standing to modify procedures, monitor the effects of changes, and lead employees through the changes. In order to be successful, the process manager needs to be skilled at negotiating, resolving conflict, managing change, and motivating others, as shown in Exhibit 8-1.

| Manager should be skilled at: | • Negotiating • Resolving conflict • Managing change • Motivating others |

Exhibit 8-1: Skills of a process manager

Responsibilities

The responsibilities of a process manager are numerous. Improvements might focus on production time or raising quality levels to meet customers' needs. Initially, the process manager needs to set improvement goals and determine measurements, so progress can be evaluated. The process manager also needs to form a process improvement team. The process manager might also need to identify subprocesses and assign managers to them.

While improvement efforts are being carried out, the process manager needs to report to management and meet with customers to ensure that their needs are being met. The process manager also needs to lead the process improvement team and communicate any business developments that could affect its work. As the process improvement proceeds, the process manager will procure resources, resolve conflicts among team members, and settle disputes among the departments that are involved.

Do it!

A-1:   Understanding process managers' responsibilities

Multiple-choice questions

1 Which of the following are among the responsibilities of a process manager?

  A   Meet with customers.

  B   Set improvement goals for the process.

  C   Provide process performance data.

  D   Select processes for improvement.

  E   Settle disputes among departments.

2 Select the qualifications needed to fulfill the role of a process manager.

  A   The skills needed to lead improvement efforts

  B   An investment in the success of improvement efforts

  C   Experience in improving other processes

  D   An advanced understanding of quality management tools

  E   Ability to meet with customers

  F   Knowledge of the process

Establishing a process improvement team

Explanation

There are five steps a process manager should use to establish a process improvement team:

1 **Identify potential candidates.** Team members must have the ability to contribute to the team. Departmental managers can help identify candidates.

2 **Meet with department heads.** The process manager should meet with all department heads involved in the process. In addition to gathering the names of potential team members, the process manager needs to build support for the improvement effort so that managers will be willing to let their employees participate and will be supportive of changes.

3 **Select team members.** Using input from departmental heads, the process manager must select the team members. Team members must understand their responsibilities.

4 **Train team members.** All members should be trained in the quality management techniques that will be used to improve the process. They should also have a thorough understanding of the goals and the boundaries of the improvement process.

5 **Initiate team activities.** As the team works to implement improvements, the process manager should prepare and lead team meetings, resolve conflict among team members, and follow up on team progress.

Do it!

A-2: Establishing a process improvement team

Exercise

1 Sequence the steps a process manager should use to establish a process improvement team.

Select team members.

Meet with all department heads involved in the process.

Train team members in the quality management techniques that will be used to improve the process.

Initiate team activities.

Identify employees who can contribute to the team.

Team members' responsibilities

Explanation

To ensure the success of a process improvement team, there are many responsibilities team members need to fulfill. Their basic responsibilities are to learn about business process improvement and attend the team's regular meetings. However, since the members of a process improvement team usually work in different departments, they also play a key role in supporting and implementing changes within their departments.

As team members begin the improvement process, they should examine how their departments affect the process. Creating flow charts of the departments' activities can be helpful. When they thoroughly understand how their departments affect the process, team members can usually determine where changes should be made.

As representatives of their departments, team members should also keep their co-workers up to date on the plans and ideas the team generates and gather feedback before any changes are made. This early communication can help avoid problems the team members themselves did not identify.

While changes are being implemented, process improvement team members play a vital role in helping their departments adjust. They can train other employees, listen to complaints, and resolve conflicts. In addition, team members can help by simply championing the improvement process and showing other employees how their work affects the process as a whole.

Topic B: Flow charts in process improvement

Explanation

Flow charts, or process flow diagrams, are used to understand a process by documenting its steps. In addition, the communication system used to carry out the process can be documented using flow charts. Understanding and analyzing the communication process can identify additional areas in need of improvement.

There are four basic flow charts symbols. Rectangles represent activities, and can be used to represent steps. Diamonds, representing decisions, should have paths proceeding from them labeled "Yes" and No." Arrows show the direction of flow, and ovals labeled "Start" and "Stop" indicate the beginning and the end of the process.

Additional flow chart symbols

For complex processes, four symbols may not be sufficient, and there are other symbols that can be helpful. *Transportation*, displayed as a large arrow, can be used to show the movement of a deliverable, as shown in Exhibit 8-2.

Exhibit 8-2: A large arrow symbol used to represent transportation

A *delay*, displayed as a half oval, represents a time when a person or product must wait. For example, a delay would occur when paperwork from one office is on hold at an interoffice mail center. *Inspection*, displayed as a large circle, can be used to represent any place in the process where an inspection must occur before the process can continue. These two symbols are shown in Exhibit 8-3.

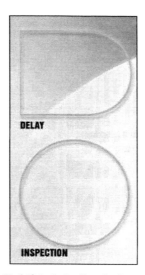

Exhibit 8-3: Symbols used to represent delay and inspection

Small circles called connectors can be used to show where a process is connected to another flow chart. This is useful when there is not enough room to complete a flow chart on a single page. Connectors are usually labeled with the same letter on both flow charts, so the connection is clear. You can determine whether a connector represents a process continued on another page or a process continued from another page by examining the arrow next to it. If the arrow is pointing toward the connector, the process is continued on another page. If the arrow is pointing away from the connector, the process is continued from another page. (See Exhibit 8-4.)

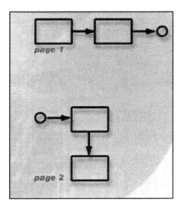

Exhibit 8-4: Small circles used as connectors

Types of flow charts

In addition to the standard flow chart, which depicts all process components, there are three other types of flow charts that can be helpful:

- Block
- Functional
- Layout

Block flow charts

Block flow charts are the easiest type to create and the most commonly used of all the types of flow charts. They provide a simple overview of an entire process. Typically, block flow charts require only activities and arrows. However, they might also include start and stop ovals. Each rectangle in a block flow chart should contain a phrase that accurately and concisely describes the activity, as shown in Exhibit 8-5.

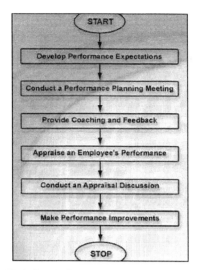

Exhibit 8-5: A sample block flow chart

Usually, these phrases start with a verb, such as, "Write key job responsibilities," and use parallel structure to allow people to process the information quickly. Sometimes, the phrases will include conditional staments, such as, "If no errors are found, print document."

Because block flow charts are used to provide a quick overview, not all of the details are always included. Block flow charts are also used to document individuals' tasks. In this case, all task details could be included within the rectangle.

Functional flow charts

The functional flow chart, which displays the person responsible for each activity and decision in the process, is another type of flow chart used for business process improvement.

Functional flow charts can also be created vertically. In Exhibit 8-6, vertical sections represent teams or individuals. The process flows from top to bottom. You should use whichever style works best with your process.

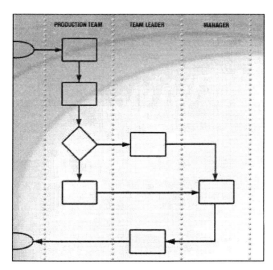

Exhibit 8-6: A vertical functional flow chart

Another variation can help to further analyze a process. By recording the process and cycle times for activities, a functional flow chart can help you determine where improvements should be made.

The *process time* is the amount of time needed to complete an activity. *Cycle time* measures the amount of time that lapses between the time an activity was last completed and the time the activity is completed again. Cycle time includes time spent waiting, transporting items, or performing any other actions that must be completed before an activity can be performed again.

To add these measurements to a functional flow chart, simply add several more columns or rows labeled "Processing Time" and "Cycle Time." Then, the measurements can be recorded in line with the activities they describe.

Analyzing processing and cycle times allows you to determine where improvements can make the most difference. By reducing processing and cycles times, you can improve a process, which ultimately improves customer satisfaction, increases sales, and improves employee morale.

Layout flow charts

Another flow chart that can be useful for business process improvement is the layout, or geographic, flow chart. This flow chart is used to show the flow of products, paper work, and other materials, as shown in Exhibit 8-7.

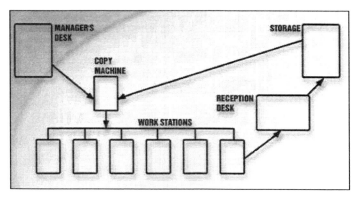

Exhibit 8-7: A sample layout flow chart

It should show a layout of a work area, including equipment, file cabinets, storage, and work stations. Arrows can then be added to show how paperwork and other materials are passed through the area. Analyzing office layout, traffic patterns, and paperwork flow allows you to determine where improvements can be made that will reduce production time. You can also reduce production time by identifying problems, such as unnecessary travel and storage delays.

Do it!

B-1: Using flow charts

Exercises

1 Select the characteristics of block flow charts.

   A They typically contain only activities and process workflow arrows.

   B They show the layout of a work area.

   C They show process and cycle times.

   D They frequently don't contain all process details.

   E They provide an overview of a complex process.

2 Which shape from the following list is used to describe each flow chart event given below: triangle, large circle, small circle, large arrow, half oval, pentagon?

   Transportation

   Connector

   Delay

   Inspection

3 Identify the four types of flow charts by matching each one to the graphic that correctly represents it.

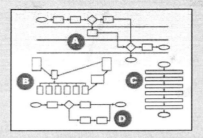

Streamlined flow chart

Mapping flow chart

Standard flow chart

Functional flow chart

Block flow chart

Layout flow chart

Unit summary: A path for change

Topic A   In this unit, you learned about the role of the **process manager** in process improvement. You learned what the qualifications are for the role, as well as its responsibilities. Then you learned how to establish a **process improvement team**, and what the responsibilities of the team members are.

Topic B   Finally, you learned that different types of flow charts can aid in business process improvement, including **block flow charts**, **functional flow charts**, and **layout flow charts**. You also learned to use several symbols for creating more advanced flow charts.

Review questions

The quality improvement initiative is underway in Icon. Managers have identified processes that can be improved and have appointed process managers to implement and oversee process change.

Don Hamilton, Game Development Coordinator in Icon's Computer Hardware and Software division, has requested a meeting with you. Don has been appointed as a process manager, with the objective of improving the development process for a top-selling game. He requests you to explain the roles and responsibilities of a process manager.

Objectives:

- Identify steps to establish a process improvement team.
- Identify responsibilities of process improvement team members.

Don is a genius at game development but weak at processes and the methodology of process improvement. The first question he asks you is what a process manager does. You decide to start from the basics. You explain that a process manager is appointed by management to oversee changes for a specific process. A lower-level manager who is closest to the process is a typical choice. The rationale behind appointing a process manager is that no single employee has a picture of the entire process. A process manager's charter is to implement change in the process as a cohesive whole.

Don inquires about the responsibilities of a process manager. You explain that a process manager is responsible for improving a process. The first step is to identify potential candidates for a process improvement team. The second step is to meet with departmental heads and ensure that the team has all required resources available to it. The third step is to select members for the team.

The fourth step is to identify goals that the team should meet. This includes defining parameters and training the team on improvement techniques. The process team is responsible for business process improvement, participating in team meetings, coming up with suggestions, and supporting and implementing changes.

The last step is to initiate team activities. This includes overseeing the team progress, resolving conflicts, and making all resources available.

Don sees the rationale behind the entire idea of process managers and process improvement teams. He asks whether a team should be composed of people from a single department or from different departments. You emphasize that a heterogeneous team works better as the team members can relate to process changes in their other departments.

Don realizes that the task of a process manager is critical to the success of process improvement.

1 How is a person selected for the role of a process manager? Select one from the following:

    a The members of the process team elect a manager.

    b The management selects a process manager through the process of elimination.

    c The management handpicks a process manager based on his or her ability to do the job.

    d The lower-level manager closest to the process is appointed by the management.

2 List the steps to select a process improvement team. (5 minutes)

3 Which of the following are responsibilities of a process improvement team? Select all that apply.

    a Plan business process improvement.

    b Apply process improvement techniques to improve a process.

    c Meet departmental heads to discuss changes in their departments.

    d Resolve intra- and inter-team conflicts.

    e Support and implement process changes in all related departments.

4 A process improvement team should be composed of individuals from different departments to prevent departmental heads from complaining of inadequate representation.

    a True

    b False

Unit 9

Implementing quality changes

Unit time: 40 minutes

Complete this unit, and you'll know how to:

A Identify the elements of a process, as well as techniques used to streamline a process.

B Measure various aspects of a process.

Topic A: Understanding processes

Explanation

Understanding a process is the only way a process improvement team can effectively improve the process. The team must understand how the process currently functions before they can identify problems. In addition, in order to understand how potential changes will affect the process, the team needs to understand specific elements of the process, as well as the process as a whole.

Process elements

There are five process elements that are important to understand:

- People
- Flow
- Effectiveness
- Efficiency
- Cost

People

One of the most important elements is the people who make the process function every day. Process improvement team members who work with the process every day can provide valuable information about their areas. However, to gain an accurate picture of the entire process, the team should gather feedback from people who work with every aspect of it.

Flow

The flow of a process is the series of actions that occur between the start and the finish. Before the process improvement team members implement any changes, they should "walk" the process and observe all the activities that comprise it. Although this can be cumbersome, it is the only way team members can gain a thorough understanding of how the process really functions.

Effectiveness

The effectiveness of a process is how well the process accomplishes what it is supposed to accomplish. The team should determine whether the process meets the needs of the internal customers at each stage and, ultimately, whether the process meets the needs of external customers.

Increasing effectiveness usually results in increased sales, improved employee morale, and enhancing customer satisfaction (as shown in Exhibit 9-1). The team should also investigate whether supplier inputs are of adequate quality, because those inputs influence the effectiveness of the process.

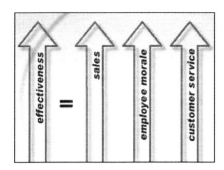

Exhibit 9-1: Results of effectiveness

Efficiency

Process efficiency is the amount of output per unit of input. There are several efficiency characteristics that the process improvement team should examine. The team should determine the cycle time and amount of wait time per unit or transaction. The team should also analyze the total cost for producing a unit to determine what percentage of the cost is due to poor quality and what percentage actually provides value to the customer.

Of the efficiency characteristics, cycle time often presents the greatest opportunity for making improvements. Some experts claim that the actual time needed to perform the work of a process is often about one percent of the total cycle time. The remaining 99 percent of the cycle time includes the time products spend waiting for another step in the process and the time used to review, rework, transport, or store the product. Reducing process cycle time can reduce costs, reduce the amount of resources used, and increase output.

Cost

Frequently, businesses record costs by department and don't examine the cost of a process as a whole. The process improvement team should examine the cost of a process as a whole, because doing so can help identify areas that are inefficient. When examining cost, the process improvement team should include the cost of every activity that is a part of the process. In addition, the team should include the overhead needed to support the process.

Do it!

A-1: Elements of a process

Multiple-choice questions

1 What's the name for the series of actions that occur between starting and finishing the process?

   A   Chain of events

   B   Action sequence

   C   Flow

   D   Developmental changes

2 What is the element of a process that makes it function everyday?

   A   Place or location

   B   People

   C   Regulations

   D   Material

Streamlining processes

Explanation

Streamlining a process involves using several quality management techniques that can help improve performance and quality. Streamlining requires the team to examine every detail of a process to search for adjustments that can help employees perform with minimum effort, while causing the fewest disturbances to the surroundings.

Techniques used to streamline a process

There are six quality management techniques that can be used to streamline a process:

- Value-added assessment
- Waste reduction
- Simplification
- Reduction of cycle time
- Standardization
- Automation

Value-added assessment

One technique is a *value-added assessment*, which is used to determine whether each activity provides value to the customer or the business. To determine whether activities provide value, think about whether they meet customers' requirements in some way. Another way to determine value is to ask whether customers would notice if the activity was not completed.

If the activity does not provide value for the customer, it might provide value for the business. Discover the purpose of the activity; and if one cannot be found, it might not be necessary. If the activity does have a purpose, ask whether the purpose is important. Frequently, activities are completed out of habit or because "that's how it's always been done."

Another way to determine whether an activity adds value is to consider whether adding more of the activity would add more value to the process. For example, adding more transportation, checks, or inspections usually does not add to the value of the process.

Waste reduction

Once the value-added activities have been identified, the process improvement team should analyze those that remain. Eliminating as many of these no-value-added activities as possible will result in *waste reduction*, another technique for streamlining processes.

Common activities that don't add value to a process include checks, inspections, administrative tasks, storage, and transportation. Checks and inspections might seem to add value to a process, but they are not truly value-added activities because continuing to add them would not continue to add value to the process. Therefore, all checks and inspections should be challenged. If a check or inspection cannot be eliminated, consider moving it to improve the flow of the process.

Administrative tasks often add unnecessary bureaucracy, work, and delays to a process. Common examples include paper work and written documentation; multiple levels of reviews, signatures, and approvals; and making, filing, and distributing copies. Each of these tasks should be carefully analyzed to determine whether it is necessary. For example, consider whether anyone ever refers to written documentation or filed copies. If they do, consider whether the frequency of use warrants the time used to create the documents.

Storage and transportation should also be minimized. To minimize storage, use just-in-time inventory systems. This practice facilitates changes by reducing the number of products that would have to be fixed if a design modification occurred. For transportation, layout flow charts can be used to analyze how a product moves through the process. Frequently, moving the location of one activity can reduce the amount of transportation.

Simplification

A third technique for streamlining a process is simplification, or reducing the number of activities in a process (as shown in Exhibit 9-2). A simpler process is easier to learn and has fewer opportunities for problems.

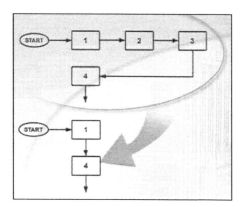

Exhibit 9-2: Process simplification by reducing the number of activities

To simplify a process, the team should identify duplicate and similar activities. Usually, duplicate activities can be eliminated, and similar activities can be combined. Before making any of these changes, the process improvement team should analyze how eliminating or combining activities would affect the rest of the process.

Another way to simplify a process is to analyze decision points, which are readily observable on a process flow chart. Identify the purpose of each decision point. If a purpose cannot be identified, the decision point is probably unnecessary. If the decision point serves a purpose, determine whether there is a way to change the process so that the need for the decision point is eliminated.

When using simplification, a process improvement team needs to keep in mind that the goal is to change the process in some way. This goal is critical, because it is possible to analyze and make changes to a flow chart without really changing the process. Remember that combining activities just by eliminating details on a process flow chart does not necessarily change how the process is performed.

Reducing cycle time

Reducing cycle time can also streamline a process. Comparing the cycle time to the actual time needed to process a product provides insight into the improvement opportunities that exist.

There are several ways to reduce cycle time, including scheduling activities parallel to one another and modifying the activity sequence. Many activities can be completed at the same time as other activities. For example, there are frequently activities in a process that can be completed parallel to automated activities.

Modifying the activity sequence can reduce cycle time in several ways. If products are moved through one area more than once, time is wasted in transportation. By examining a layout flow chart of the process, excessive transportation can be identified. Frequently, the process can be streamlined by changing the activity sequence so that products follow the simplest route through the process.

Another way that adjusting the activity sequence can reduce cycle time is by ensuring that time-based activities are completed to meet specific deadlines. For example, suppose the last interdepartmental mail pick-up is at three o'clock. Any documents completed after that time would not be mailed until the following day. Adjusting the activity sequence could allow all documents needing to be sent to other departments to be completed by three o'clock, which would eliminate the delay.

Standardization

Standardization should not be used until the value-added assessment, waste reduction, simplification, and reduction of cycle time techniques have been completed. This sequence is important because only processes that have been streamlined should be standardized.

Standardization is the process of teaching employees the correct way to complete the streamlined process. Using standardization ensures that all employees understand the changes that have been made and are completing all of the activities in the same manner. Therefore, standardization is a common technique for reducing the variation in a process.

To provide employees with the information they need, the process needs to be documented with a flow chart. Doing so can help employees quickly and easily understand how the process should be completed. Checklists can also help ensure that work is completed as planned, or to document who completed the work and when. In addition, common forms should be produced based upon templates, so every employee produces them the same way.

Automation

Automation can increase the speed at which many activities are completed. Process improvement teams should look for areas in a process in which automation could be implemented. It is important to note that automation takes place only after the other streamlining techniques have been applied. Rushing to implement an automated solution can result in a process that produces more errors at a faster rate than the manual process produced.

There are two common types of activities that can benefit from automation. Repetitive activities often can be completed faster by a computer than by a person. If completing the activities more quickly will benefit the process, automation might be a helpful improvement.

In addition, automation can improve communication among areas of the process that are physically separated. For example, some computer systems can manage inventories by identifying which warehouse has the needed materials, which is faster than humans tracking the inventory and communicating the information.

Do it!

A-2: Streamlining a process

Exercises

1 Select the characteristic that is a part of the simplification technique of streamlining.

  A Reducing the number of activities.

  B Analyzing whether activities meet customers' needs.

  C Scheduling activities parallel to one another.

  D Challenging checks and inspections.

2 Match the streamlining techniques in the following list to the descriptions given below: Standardization; Reduction of cycle time; Waste reduction; Simplification; Automation.

  Eliminating checks, inspections, or administrative tasks.

  Scheduling activities parallel to one another.

  Providing checklists to help employees complete their work.

3 Match the streamlining techniques in the following list to the description given below: simplification; value-added assessment; waste reduction; activity dispersal; automation.

  Analyzing whether individual activities are necessary to meet customers' needs

  Analyzing or eliminating decision points

  Completing repetitive activities at a faster rate

4 Discuss the functional process flow map given below.

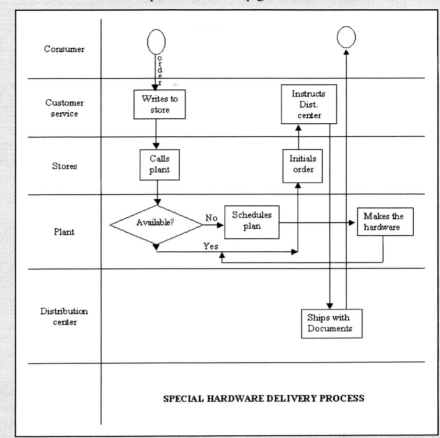

SPECIAL HARDWARE DELIVERY PROCESS

5 How can you streamline the process depicted in the above diagram? Discuss.

Topic B: Measuring processes

Explanation

How a process is measured can determine the benefit gained from the measurements. For example, many processes are measured only at their ends. This practice provides little feedback about the individual activities that employees perform, and any feedback provided is too late to be helpful. Measurements should be established that provide feedback as soon as an activity is completed. Doing so provides employees with immediate, relevant feedback, and prevents problems from growing by identifying them as they occur.

What should be measured?

Any activity that significantly affects the efficiency or effectiveness of a process should be measured. By establishing measurements for these activities, management communicates to employees that these activities are critical. Other activities that are important to measure include those that directly affect the satisfaction of an internal customer and those that consume large amounts of resources. In addition, any features or characteristics that are important to the external customer should be measured. For example, if accuracy is very important to the external customer, then management should find a way to measure it.

Do it!

B-1: Measuring a process

Multiple-choice questions

1 Select the main goal of establishing measurements in business process improvements.

   A To measure the percent of value-added activities

   B To measure the process performance

   C To measure employee performance

   D To measure cycle time

2 Which aspects of a process should be measured?

   A Characteristics affecting external customer satisfaction

   B Activities affecting efficiency or effectiveness

   C Activities consuming large amounts of resources

   D Activities requiring supplier inputs

   E Features needing extra testing

   F Activities affecting internal customer satisfaction

Importance of measuring process performance

Explanation

Measuring process performance is important, because controlling a process is nearly impossible without measurements. Measuring a process can provide regular feedback on its performance so that any changes can be identified and investigated as soon as possible.

Measurements are also important for employees who work with the process every day. Without feedback about their performance, employees can lose motivation. However, remember that the goal is to measure the process. If employees feel that all measurements taken are used to gauge their performance, they are not likely to report the measurements accurately. Management should emphasize that the main goal of the measurements is to determine the performance of the process.

It is also important to consider what aspects of the process are measured. Employees sometimes feel that if something is not measured, management doesn't care about it. Similarly, employees might put more emphasis on activities that are measured, even if those activities are not essential to the process. For example, if management only measures cycle time, the cycle time is likely to improve, but cost and quality might suffer. A common phrase used in quality management is "What gets measured gets done." Therefore, management should measure all important process characteristics.

Do it!

B-2:   Understanding the importance of measurement

Exercises

1 Select all the reasons why it is important to measure process performance.

   A   Hard data is all that matters.

   B   Employees need to know that their work is being measured.

   C   Measurement helps show employees which aspects of the process management considers important.

   D   Changes in measured performance can help point to the need for process improvement.

2 Discuss the types of measurement that exist in a process at your company. Do these measurements add value for internal or external customers? Why or why not?

Unit summary: Implementing quality changes

Topic A

In this unit, you learned that five important elements of a process are **people**, **flow**, **effectiveness**, **efficiency**, and **cost**. You also learned about several techniques for **streamlining** a process, and the importance of **standardization** after you do.

Topic B

Finally, you learned how to select the aspects of a process to measure, and why measurement is important.

Review questions

John Cunningham is the Quality Control Manager for Icon's Computer Hardware and Software Division. You have asked to meet with John because he is very knowledgeable about process evaluation and how to implement quality changes.

You want to learn more about these topics because your team has recently experienced the failure of a new educational game called L'Attitude. As the Product Development Coordinator in charge of this software, it is your job to determine what went wrong in the development and marketing processes.

By identifying the elements of a process, the quality management techniques that can be used to streamline a process, and the aspects of a process that can be measured, you hope to determine what mistakes were made in the creation of L'Attitude and correct those errors immediately.

1 What do you call the financial aspect of the process that you should examine?

   a Cost

   b Allowance

   c Financial plan

   d Allocation of resources

2 What is the term for how well the process accomplishes what it is supposed to accomplish?

   a Productivity

   b Effectiveness

   c Performance

   d Resourcefulness

3 What process element has to do with the amount of output per unit of input?

   a Quantity to quality ratio

   b Processing power

   c Expected effect

   d Efficiency

4 Identify a technique that can be used to streamline a process.

   a Reduced pre-launch period

   b Expanded testing phase

   c Reduction of cycle time

   d Increase in research and development time

5 Which of the following techniques is used to reduce the number of activities in your process?

   a Refinement

   b Omission

   c Elimination

   d Simplification

6 Which technique would you used to determine whether your process benefits your customers and your business?

   a Discovery

   b Process inspection

   c Cost/ benefit assessment

   d Value-added assessment

7 What do you call the streamlining technique in which you improve the flow of the process by analyzing non-value-added activities and eliminating or moving them?

   a Process reconstruction

   b Waste management

   c Waste reduction

   d Process reorganization

8 What technique might you use if you discover that you need to increase the speed with which activities in your process are completed?

   a Automation

   b Operation

   c Machination

   d Locomotion

9 Identify the last step for streamlining a process, through which employees learn the right way to complete their tasks.

   a Standardization

   b Codification

   c Promulgation

   d Indoctrination

10 Why is it important to measure process performance?

   a Regular feedback about the performance of the process allows changes to be identified and investigated as soon as possible.

   b Regular feedback about the personnel involved in the process aids in measuring their performance.

   c Regular feedback about the outcome or results of the process helps management know who to blame for mistakes and errors.

   d Regular feedback about the tasks, steps, or phases of a process enables management to compare it to competitors' processes.

11 When should processes be measured?

   a As soon as an activity is completed

   b When you suspect something is wrong with the process

   c On an as-needed basis

   d After the entire process is completed

12 What aspects of a process should be measured?

   a Any activity that significantly affects the efficiency or effectiveness of a process

   b The most difficult or complicated activities

   c The activities in which there is the most potential for error or flaws

   d The activities for which newest employees and least skilled employees are responsible

Quality Management

Course summary

This summary contains information to help you bring the course to a successful conclusion. Using this information, you will be able to:

A Use the summary text to reinforce what you've learned in class.

B Determine the next courses in this series (if any), as well as any other resources that might help you continue to learn about Quality Management.

Topic A: Course summary

Use the following summary text to reinforce what you've learned in class. It is not intended as a script, but rather as a starting point.

Quality Management

Unit 1

In this unit, you learned the concepts commonly associated with **Quality management**, the **role of management** in implementing quality, and the steps an organization should follow to incorporate **improvements** into daily management. You also learned the ways in which **variation** leads to loss, the characteristics of **common causes** of variation, and the frequent sources of variation.

Unit 2

In this unit, you learned about the relationship between **quality and cost**. You also learned about the importance of quality requirements, and the **1-10-100 rule**. Finally, you learned about management's responsibility for achieving **conformance**, and the costs of **customer dissatisfaction**.

Unit 3

In this unit, you learned about the characteristics of a **customer-oriented organization**, the steps for becoming customer-oriented, and approaches for conducting customer research. You also learned the benefits of developing a customer orientation, benefits of satisfying customers, and the financial incentives of developing **loyal customers**.

Unit 4

In this unit, you learned how to create **flow charts**, including the symbols used in them. You learned about the benefits of using flow charts, and about different types of flow charts. Next, you learned how to create different types of **check sheets** and how to avoid data collection pitfalls. You also learned how to create and interpret various types of **histograms**. Then you learned how to create **run charts**, and to identify common patterns in them, such as **cycles**, **mixtures**, **trends**, and **shifts**. Finally, you learned about the main components of a **control chart** and their importance.

Unit 5

In this unit, you learned how to create several kinds of **cause-and-effect** diagrams. Next, you learned how to use **Pareto charts** to prioritize problems or problem causes. Then, you learned how to use **scatter diagrams** to analyze relationships between variables, and to determine the strength of correlation between variables. Finally, you learned how to create an **interrelationship** diagram to analyze the events that lead to a problem.

Unit 6

In this unit, you learned to use the **brainstorming process** to generate a large number of ideas quickly. Next, you learned how to create **affinity diagrams** in order to generate and categorize ideas for solving problems. Then, you learned how to construct **activity network** diagrams, which help to plan improvement efforts. You also learned about two techniques for **network planning**, **CPM** and **PERT**. Finally, you learned how to identify the **critical path** and **critical activities** in a process.

Unit 7

In this unit, you learned about **management's responsibilities** in business process improvement. You learned that management must determine the processes that need to be improved, communicate the importance of initiatives to employees, update employees on progress, resolve conflicts, and evaluate the process after improvements have been implemented. You also learned how to plan for improvements, and the criteria for selecting a process.

Unit 8

In this unit, you learned about the qualifications and responsibilities of a **process manager**. You learned the criteria for selecting a process improvement team, and team members' responsibilities. Finally, you learned about the use of **block flow charts**, **functional flow charts**, and **layout flow charts** for business process improvement.

Unit 9

In this unit, you learned that the five elements important in understanding a process are **people**, **flow**, **effectiveness**, **efficiency**, and **cost**. You also learned about techniques for **streamlining** a process, including **value-added assessment**, **Waste reduction**, **simplification**, **reduction of cycle time**, **standardization**, and **automation**. Finally, you learned about the importance of **measuring** processes and **process performance**, as well as how to select the aspects of a process that should be measured.

Topic B: Continued learning after class

It is impossible to learn to use any subject effectively in a single day. To get the most out of this class, it is important that you begin making use of the Quality Management techniques you've learned as soon as possible. Course Technology also offers resources for continued learning.

Next courses in this series

This is the only course in this series.

Other resources

Course Technology's sister company, NETg, offers a full line of online and computer-based courses on Quality Management and a variety of other subjects. For more information, visit www.netg.com. This course maps precisely to the following three NETg courses:

- *Quality Management: The Quality Management Process*
- *Quality Management: Quality Management Tools*
- *Quality Management: Business Process Improvement*

Glossary

Activity

A step in a process. In flow charts, activities are displayed as rectangles.

Activity network diagrams

A diagram in which a project is divided into a series of activities. Activity network diagrams are used for planning implementation of quality improvements and other projects.

Activity-on-arrow method

A method of creating activity network diagrams in which arrows represent activities, while rectangles called nodes represent events and demonstrate how activities are related.

Activity-on-node method

A method of creating activity network diagrams in which boxes called nodes represent activities, while arrows drawn between the nodes represent activity relationships.

Affinity diagrams

A type of diagram that is used by a team of five to 15 members to create a large number of ideas for solving a problem, as well as to organize those ideas into categories.

Appraisal costs

Costs related to inspections of raw materials, work-in-process materials, and end products.

Bell curve

A graph shape, common in Histograms, that is symmetrical with a single peak in the middle.

Benchmarking

Learning how other companies perform specific processes. Used to gain ideas for improving or overhauling the way a company performs the process.

Block flow charts

A flow chart showing a simple overview of an entire process, typically requiring only activities and arrows. They can also include start and stop ovals.

Brainstorming

A process that helps generate many ideas in a small amount of time. Brainstorming works best when used by a group of four to nine people.

Cause-and-effect diagrams

Diagrams used to identify and categorize the possible causes of a problem and to help discover its root. Also known as fishbone or Ishikawa diagrams.

Check sheets

Used to record the frequency of occurrence of various events.

Comment cards

Used to collect specific information about customer satisfaction.

Connectors

Small circles that show where a process depicted on a flow chart is connected to another flow chart.

Control charts

Used to provide a running record of a process, helping determine when a process is running smoothly and when it needs attention.

Critical Path Method (CPM)

A schedule development technique used to identify the least flexible activities in a project based on float calculations.

Critical path

In a CPM or PERT chart, the longest chain of activities that cannot be completed concurrently.

Customers

Any individuals or groups to whom you provide products or services.

Customer exciters

Unexpected surprises or features used to generate strong but temporary interest in customers.

Customer loyalty

The feeling that a customer wants to continue doing business with an organization. To achieve customer loyalty, a company must provide consistently good service, it must provide something more than what the competition provides, and it must build a relationship with customers over time.

Customer orientation

An organizational mindset in which meeting the needs of the customer becomes an organization's focus.

Customer research

Regularly gathering feedback to understand customers' changing needs and wants.

Cycle time

The amount of time that lapses between the time an activity was last completed and the time the activity is completed again.

Decision point

A point in a process at which decisions must be made before the process can continue, displayed as a diamond in a flow chart.

Delay

At point in a process at which a person or product must wait, displayed as a half oval in a flow chart.

Empowerment

Giving employees flexibility in their interactions to enable them to better serve customers.

External failure costs

Costs that arise when defects are found by the customer.

Flow charts (process flow diagrams)

Used to understand a process by documenting its steps and the relationships between them.

Focus groups

A formal means of gathering information with a group of five to ten customers.

Functional flow chart

A type of flow chart that shows who is responsible for each activity and decision in the process.

Histograms

A type of bar chart that shows variation in a set of data.

Inspection

A point in a process at which an inspection must occur before the process can continue, displayed as a large circle in a flow chart.

Internal failure costs

Costs that arise when defects are found before a product reaches the customer.

Interrelationship diagrams

A type of cause-and-effect diagram used to analyze the events that lead to a problem (also known as interrelationship diagraphs).

Interviews

One-on-one discussions with a customer.

Layout flow charts

Used to show the flow of products, paperwork, and other materials (also known as geographic flow charts).

Lower control limit

In a control charts, the statistically-determined lower boundary of expected process performance.

Pareto chart

A type of bar chart used to prioritize problems or problem causes.

Pareto Principle

A guideline stating that roughly 80 percent of effects are produced by 20 percent of the causes. Pareto charts are based on this principle, named for the nineteenth-century Italian economist Vilfredo Pareto.

Predecessors

In an activity network diagram, activities that must be finished before others begin.

Prevention costs

Cost that arise from initiatives to prevent defects in products, such as evaluations of suppliers, employee training, and other plans made for achieving quality.

Price of conformance (POC)

The cost of doing things right the first time.

Price of non-conformance (PONC)

The cost of not doing things right the first time.

Process

Any work you, a group, or a company performs.

Process efficiency

The amount of output per unit of input.

Process time

The amount of time needed to complete an activity.

Process variation

The fluctuation of process performance.

Program Evaluation and Review Technique (PERT)

A schedule development technique used to determine project duration based on three time estimates: optimistic, pessimistic, and most likely.

Questionnaires

A way to gather customer input when customers are not close enough to allow for focus groups or interviews.

Run chart

Used to show variation of a process characteristic over time.

Scatter diagram

Type of chart used to determine whether a relationship exists between two variables of a process.

Stable process

A process that will continue to provide predictable results unless something changes.

Standardization

The process of teaching employees the correct way to complete a streamlined process.

Standards

Guidelines for performing specific tasks.

Successors

In an activity network diagram, activities that can begin only after the start or completion of one or more other activities.

Transportation

Show movement of a deliverable, displayed as a large arrow in a flow chart.

Upper control limit

In control charts, the statistically-determined upper boundary of expected process performance.

Value-added assessment

A technique for streamlining processes by determining whether each activity provides value to the customer or the business.

Waste reduction

A technique for streamlining processes in which no-value-added activities are eliminated.

Index